Sharon Becker

You Can Make Money From Your Hobby

You Can Make Money From Your Hobby

Building a Business Doing What You Love

Martha Campbell Pullen, Ph.D.
with Lilly Walters

BROADMAN
&HOLMAN
PUBLISHERS

Nashville, Tennessee

0-7394-0263-3

Published by Broadman & Holman Publishers, Nashville, Tennessee
Editorial Team: Vicki Crumpton, Janis Whipple, Kim Overcash
Typesetting: Desktop Miracles, Dallas, TX

PREFACE

For nothing is impossible with God.
—Luke 1:37

Occasionally when I tell people about how my business evolved, they ask, "How did you do all that?" The answer is that God has done all of it and I give him complete credit. I couldn't have done it without him. Period. The Bible is my number one comfort, and when I have sense enough to pray rather than try to work things out myself, I fare much better.

I would quickly add that I had the support of my husband and my children. Joe paid the bills for our family the first years when I drew no salary, and he contributed several times to paying the company bills so I could keep on going. My children not only helped me with the business, they ate a lot of spaghetti all weekend and soup during the week because there was no time to cook.

My parents and Joe's parents helped me unbelievably. They took care of the children whenever they could; they invited us to eat or cooked and brought food over to last several days. I hired all the help I could afford for child care as well as for help with some of my housework and laundry. We didn't buy new cars, I certainly did not buy clothes for myself, we didn't do "wonderful vacations," and we did not paint the walls or get new carpet. We couldn't even afford to hire outside carpet cleaners so I rented one at the local Winn Dixie.

When I opened my retail store, I realized that some activities in my life had to go if I were to put God first, family second, and business third. First, I resigned from all of the secular volunteer organizations to which I belonged. However, I remained in my job as a GA leader in our church. Second, we quit giving parties and going to them. Third, we eliminated almost all social activities other than family ones, even on Friday and Saturday nights. We realized that family time meant just that— TIME. There wasn't much time after working the way we were working, and all non-business time must go to family. If we went to a movie, we took our youngest, Joanna, and her friends. We loved to stay at home on Saturday night and read books and spend time with Joanna. Since the boys were teens at this time, they certainly did not want to go to a movie with us or stay home and read on a Saturday night!

Let me hasten to add that I did not start the massive international travel until Joanna was in the ninth grade. My boys were then grown and away from home. Several good things came from my intensive travel. Joanna and her dad became best friends. I had always hovered over my only little girl, so I guess I hadn't left much room for father/daughter time.

My social friends became the people with whom I worked. My ministry became bringing joy to women through teaching and sharing our beloved sewing. Part of this joy came from supporting and listening to people who were hurting. I know God doesn't need me; however, I hope he chooses to use me through this sewing business.

I pray that this book will motivate people to ask God's guidance in showing them how to start a business if it really is his will. Secondly, this book is to show people how to begin and operate a small business. Thirdly, this is the story of how God allowed *me* to do just that. I will quickly add that it is also Lilly Walter's story, since God opened the door for her to assist me with this book.

I thank God for the opportunity to write this book. I pray that it will be an inspiration to you in your journey toward your own business. In closing I would offer you Philippians 4:13, "I can do all things through Christ who strengthens me" (NKJV).

CONTENTS

For more information:

Martha Pullen Co., Inc.
518 Madison St.
Huntsville, Ala., 35801
256-533-9586, 800-547-4176

Lilly Walters, Executive Director
Walters International Speakers Services
P.O. Box 1120, Glendora, Calif., 91740
626-335-8069, fax 626-335-6127

E-mail us through our on-line addresses:
mpullen446@aol.com
Lilly@Walters-Intl.com

INTRODUCTION

Turn Your Passions into Profits

What would your life be like if you could spend all day—every day—doing what you are passionate about?

Yes, yes, I hear you giggling! You're thinking, "Sure! I could spend all day on the golf course . . . shopping at Nieman Marcus . . . drinking a lemonade on the beach in Tahiti . . . etc."

Really?

Let's say you got to indulge in your favorite fantasy for a few weeks. Come now, be honest, those fun playtime activities start to lose their attraction.

> The success of an entrepreneur is to do that for which you have an enduring passion.

After you have had your fill of "that," what would your favorite day-in-and-day-out indulgences be? Ah! Now *that* is what you are truly passionate about! And enduring passion is what you will need to bring your dreams to reality.

I combined all the things I was truly passionate about and created a multi-million-dollar business. And it all started with smocking! (You're giggling again.) For those of you who are domestically-challenged, smocking is a type of needlework in which the embroidery is stitched onto very small pleats or gathers, forming a kind of honeycomb ornamentation.

I built a successful business by doing the things I am passionate about: creating beauty for my family and friends, working with people, teaching, sewing, my love of smocking and other forms of heirloom sewing. The result is a flourishing business and an abundance of life I didn't realize was possible!

How We Will Travel through This Book

People look at our multi-million-dollar business, the international magazine, the national TV show, and think, "That must have been easy! She just took her hobby and simply started making money with it!"

You know, it is simple. So simple it seems complicated. Lilly and I have divided this book into four sections—four simple fabrics that we quilted together for profiting from your hobby: The Possibilities, The Plan, The Promotion, and The People Skills . . . with GRACE!

Part 1—The Possibilities: Exploring the Many Ways to Profit from Your Hobby. We will explore hundreds of ways other hobbyists have taken their dreams and turned them into profit-making businesses. We'll help you decide how to best turn your home into a starting place to launch your hobby business. You will be wise to decide when you will hire staff, get a "real" office, and buy copy machines before you ever launch into making money from your hobby.

> *People with goals succeed because they*
> *know where they're going.*
> —Earl Nightingale

Part 2—The Plan: Going from Free to Fee. We'll give you some ideas to develop a business plan, work the plan, and plan your office space in your home. Then we'll give you help on what to do when your plans fail and how to create new plans!

> *. . . those who plan good have joy.*
> —Proverbs 12:20, RSV

Part 3—The Promotion: Creating Visibility. As the word implies—pro-*motion*! Your product and service do no good sitting at home! Advertising is out of the financial reach of most of us when we begin. However, successful marketing is often a matter of creativity! We will explore ways to get your business in motion and to go from little to legendary! Creating flyers, newsletters, limited editions, holiday packages, giving seminars and speeches will be covered, and more!

> *Webster's Dictionary says "promotion is to move*
> *forward, raise, contribute to growth and prosperity."*
> *The opposite is "demotion."*
> *You know which way that will take you!*
> —Dottie Walters, author, speaker, and
> self-made millionaire from the
> business she started in her garage

Part 4—The People: Likability, Loyalty, and Leadership Skills. Once you begin to make money with your hobby, you will quickly discover you need people working for you. You cannot succeed alone; you must have a team of loyal customers and loyal staff. Your people skills are every bit as important as your knowledge of your product or service. You cannot buy loyalty; you cannot buy enthusiasm; you cannot buy the hearts and minds of people—these things you must earn. We will explore the ways to earn the loyalty of your customers and staff and keep it, starting with ways you can become more personally likeable and finishing with problem-solving skills.

*Harry Gordon Selfridge developed a large
department store chain in London. He told
about two different kinds of executives.
"A boss drives other people; a leader coaches them.
A boss loves to use authority; a leader prefers goodwill.
A boss always says 'I'; a leader uses 'we.'"*
—Adapted from *Speaker's Library of
Business* by Joe Griffith

We Do It with Grace

Grace is a wonderful word. It makes one think of beauty, harmony, attractiveness, quality, goodwill, and mercy—traits that will enrich all aspects of your personal and business life. It can also mean a perception of what is appropriate, as in, "That saleswoman has the grace to ask about my children every time we meet." For me as a Christian, the most important meaning of grace is that entrance into the kingdom of heaven is by God's grace alone. Grace is really all about God's generosity.

God's generous "grace" represents the main element of my own success. My success is indeed a gift from God. It is he that has given me all of the skills to build this business. It is he who has picked up the pieces over and over and fixed things. It is he who has given me these wonderful employees to make the whole thing happen. I give God all of the credit and thank him for such generosity.

As you embark upon the journey into a new business, or as you look for ways to make your old business more profitable, please, do so with grace and graciousness. Grace is such a beautiful word with such life-changing significance; therefore, Lilly and I have chosen to weave and stitch this whole book around the five letters G.R.A.C.E. When I teach, I use GRACE as an acronym:

God: He is first in all things. I gave my business to God, and when I did it became successful. Creating and maintaining a business has been called a "rat race." Sadly for many, that is all too true; that first joy of turning their hobby into profits is gone. But add God to that "RACE" and you achieve GRACE. Shortly after I began my business I discovered that God could and would be my business partner. Although I had been a churchgoer all my life and I had come from a Christian family, I had not indeed accepted Christ as my Savior. Through God's grace I became a Christian and nothing has been the same since. That happened shortly after I opened my business. Facing the financial difficulties of the first years of business would have been too much for me to face alone. I began to search the Bible for Scriptures with God's promises in this area of my life. My favorite Scripture when facing difficult times in business is James 1:2–4: "Consider it pure joy, my brothers, whenever you face trials of many kinds, because you know that the testing of your faith develops perseverance. Perseverance must finish its work so that you may be mature and complete, not lacking anything."

Resilience: Get up when you're down. You conquer by continuing. Work. Then work some more. Add to this quilt personal enthusiasm and the other fabrics we discussed, and you'll have a joyous and thriving business.

Action: It is not enough to dream—wake up and work at it! We will explore many ways for you to take action today and make money tomorrow with your hobby.

Creativity: Allow the unusual to happen. Look around you— the tools you need for a wonderful idea to turn your avocation into profit may be lying right there at your feet, just waiting for you to discover it.

Enthusiasm: Allow the spirit of excitement to fill you and spread to your friends. It is contagious and delightfully enriching. Andrew Carnegie wrote, "People who are unable to motivate themselves must be content with mediocrity, no matter how impressive their other talents."

Other than God, each of the attributes of GRACE are nothing alone. Our enthusiasms are nothing without well-thought-out planning. The most brilliant, innovative creative ideas are no doubt still sitting idle in people's minds because the dreamer didn't have the resilience to push them through to their birth in the marketplace. You need all five attributes of GRACE to be a success in small business.

The high prize in life, the crowning fortune of man,
is to be born with a bias to some pursuit which finds
him in employment and happiness.
—Ralph Waldo Emerson

PART 1

THE POSSIBILITIES

*Exploring the Many Ways to
Profit from Your Hobby*

---

*If I were to wish for anything, I should not wish
for wealth and power, but for the passionate
sense of the potential, for the eye which, ever
young and ardent, sees the possible. Pleasure
disappoints, possibility never.*
> —Søren Kierkegaard (1813–55),
> Danish philosopher

In this part of our book I hope to inspire you and help open
your mind to the thousands of opportunities available to you in
many fields. We'll discuss many ways you can turn your own
beloved hobby into a profit-making venture, and how to decide
if the ideas you generate are right for you.

CHAPTER ONE

From Passion to Profit: Martha's Story

Why does it take us so long to follow our heart's desires? I read an article that said that most of us should go into a profession for which we showed talent and interest as a child. It took me years to discover the truth of this. When I was only five or six years old, my Aunt Chris began to let me make Christmas stockings and doll clothes. My mama was a wonderful seamstress who taught me basic sewing, and in high school I took home economics from my wonderful mentor Mrs. Ingram. I have always been passionate about sewing and I still am. But I didn't yet have enough experiences with the darks and lights of life to follow what I loved doing most.

Good Times, Bad Times

University of Alabama. Bear Bryant was the coach and Joe Namath the star of the team. January 1, 1963, was the date that we won the Orange Bowl in Miami and an unusual set of circumstances led to my meeting President Kennedy in his box at the game. Newspaper headlines featured pictures of me crying for joy as I was introduced to the President of the United States. I graduated cum laude in education in 1965, and was even elected president of the College of Education. I married a great guy. My world was speeding along with the lights, glamour, and success.

Then my world crashed; darkness set in. Divorced with two little boys, I had no job, no health insurance, an old car, and no money. I was able to find a teaching job in Atlanta. But living in Atlanta was expensive; my salary, after taxes, was $395, my rent was $250, and my car payment was $87 per month! My child support only paid for child care. We didn't have enough for food and gas for me to drive to my job each day. I prayed that the children wouldn't get sick because a visit to the doctor and medicine would put me without any food and gas money for the rest of the month. However, God took good care of me and my family. I was shown ways to make it through. When my children were sick, I would leave my house at 3:30 in the morning and drive halfway to Scottsboro where my mama and daddy would meet me and pick up the sick child. They would take him to the doctor and stay with him while he needed to be out of school.

I remember those days like they were yesterday. I also remember when I only had bread, Cream of Wheat, frozen pot pies, and peanut butter in my kitchen. I remember my oldest son going to my sister's house, opening the refrigerator and saying, "Mama, Aunt Mary is rich. She has a whole refrigerator full of food."

I thought many times, *I'll get a Ph.D. if it kills me and never have to live like this again. I'll work twenty-four hours a day if necessary to be able to go to the grocery store anytime I like! I'll never have my children wear too short, worn-out pants again. I will figure out how to make enough money to succeed.*

Luckily my two boys were very young and they didn't care that their clothes were too short and worn out. I also vowed that by the time they wanted nice clothes I would be in a financial position to buy them. I unfortunately did not share my boys' nonchalant attitude toward clothes. I would walk through Rich's and Lord and Taylor in Atlanta and think as I looked at the good-looking outfits, *One day I won't be poor anymore. I'll get more education which will enable me to have a few gorgeous clothes.*

I had not yet accepted God into my life, but he was planting seeds in my soul that would one day grow into a life full of

GRACE. In the meanwhile, my sewing and stitching skills helped see me through that time and gave me clothes to wear during my divorced years.

Meeting Joe

The second most exciting thing in my life happened on October 2, 1974. I met Joe. God moves in such mysterious ways sometimes. Having been hired to do some consulting with the Army, I was traveling to Huntsville late one afternoon when a crown fell off my front tooth. I absolutely had to find a dentist. I drove around Huntsville Hospital looking for a dental office only to realize that it was 7 o'clock at night. Finally, I saw a sign which said Dental Lab so I pulled in. The lights were on. I pushed on the door and met the dentist—Joe. The rest is history. We married on December 30, 1974. The last twenty-three years have been the best of my life.

Some Soul-Searching

God provided an assistantship to attend graduate school full-time at the University of Alabama. This was an answer to prayer. After finishing my Ph.D., I had a wonderful job teaching in the teacher education department at Athens State College. I was blessed to have exciting students. I was at the beginning of making a decent salary and had excellent benefits. I had the job I had once dreamed of back in graduate school. My consulting business was beginning to soar.

So what was wrong with my life?

The one big problem was that I had to drive one hour to Athens to work and one hour home each day. Athens had mostly commuter students who needed night classes. That necessitated my leaving Huntsville about one o'clock in the afternoon and arriving home after 11 P.M. I had five children, one of them a toddler. None of my boys were old enough to drive a car. All had to be transported home from school and to other activities in the afternoon.

My husband can't cook and everybody was hungry around six in the evening. My three-year-old daughter needed to go to bed reasonably early and I never got to see her at night. Although I hired excellent help in my home, the situation just wasn't working. I didn't want to miss time with my family in the evenings, and driving alone for an hour after 10 P.M. wasn't pleasing to me or my family.

Joe and I began to really search our souls to answer the question, "Is this teaching job really worth it, considering the sacrifices that our family is making?" We concluded that we would rather live on less money and have me at home with the family. Although I knew I would miss my students and my colleagues, I resigned.

Colors Seen by Candlelight

Without a mentally demanding job to keep my mind occupied, I was starting to dream. Through the lights and darks I was experiencing in my life, I could barely see beautiful colors—vaguely, as if by candlelight. Elizabeth Barrett Browning wrote,

> "Yes," I answered you last night;
> "No," this morning, sir, I say:
> Colors seen by candle-light
> Will not look the same by day.

I thought the light of day would dim my dream of owning my own business. Yet in the light of days that followed, this dream just got brighter.

I began to ask myself, *What do you want to be when you grow up?* I still loved to sew more than any other hobby, so I decided I would rather try and fail than not try at all. Joe assured me that he could support the family while I tried this business. We told ourselves that we would not starve if we used our life savings to buy the first inventory. On August 1, 1981, I followed my dream to open a simple little smocking shop.

Beginning of Light

About three years after opening my business, that simple little smocking shop was anything but. I had expanded very quickly to a large business and had cash flow growing pains. I had written my first book which was a best seller, but things still looked bleak.

I spent the first five years with no salary at all and we sold property twice to pay the bills. I had left the financial stability that I had worked so hard to achieve. There was a great deal of darkness. Luckily Joe was able to support our family for those five years. The next five years, my salary was only in the hundreds of dollars per month. That alone was also depressing. During those ten years, I dissolved into tears many nights telling Joe that I thought we had better sell the inventory and quit. He believed in me enough to help me pay the bills once more and keep me going.

On the other hand, there were many positives in my business. We were expanding by writing more books. We were going to more markets to sell our wholesale goods. We were starting new businesses, such as *Sew Beautiful* magazine. However, we were investing much more quickly than the money was coming in. The staff grew larger but the profits just weren't there yet. Were we spreading my good news of bringing sewing back into many women's lives? Yes. Was the business growing? Yes. Was I getting paid for my work? Not monetarily. Was I depressed? Absolutely!

How GRACE Came to Our Business

If any of you lacks wisdom, he should ask God,
who gives generously to all without finding fault,
and it will be given to him.
—James 1:5

To say that I lacked wisdom in running a business is an understatement. My only "business experience" had been selling clothing and jewelry when I was in the ninth grade at my Uncle Albert's store.

Although I had been a member of a church all of my life, somehow I was too thickheaded to really hear God's Word which was presented to me on a regular basis. In April 1983, I became a Christian but a true baby Christian. I knew that God had completely brought a new joy and a new life to me, but I knew nothing about his promises. I had learned that Jesus died on the cross that I might go to heaven; however, I didn't know about his personal power to help me with my business. I began to study the Bible. In December 1984, I was nearly in tears about how I was going to pay the bills. I owed the Swiss fabric company $23,000 and I had $100 in my business account. December is a low month in the sewing business so I knew that I wouldn't sell much and certainly wouldn't collect much from my wholesale customers, since their businesses would be as bad as mine.

I had around $50,000 on my accounts receivable, but my customers usually took ninety days to pay and sometimes I had to call them several times before they would send even a partial payment. At church that Sunday, our pastor made a statement that we could give not only our successes but also our failures to God and he would take them. That was a revelation to me. Did that mean I could give him my entire business—the good and the bad? Joe encouraged me to give God my failures and ask him to handle them for me. The next Monday, I gave my business to God. I gave him the wonderful part of bringing happiness and stress relief to customers; and, more importantly, I gave him the complete financial disaster that it was that month.

Casting all your care upon him, for he careth for you.
—1 Peter 5:7, KJV

As I prayed, I began to have a beautiful peace about the whole situation. I prayed that if this business weren't his will for my life, that I would be willing to do whatever he wanted me to do. If my sewing business was God's will, I asked him, very directly, to fix my finances so I wouldn't go crazy with worry.

The week after I gave the business to God and began to wait on his direction, I realized that if God were to choose to pull it out of the water, I had better ask specifically for an amount that was necessary to pay Switzerland so they would send me more goods for Easter, which is our good season. Although I now understand that God knew every penny that I needed and when I needed it, in 1983 I didn't know that. So I began to pray, "God, I need $23,000 to wire to Switzerland so they can release my new order for fabric. Please let my customers pay *me* first this time." I didn't ask for a miracle for new sales, but rather I asked specifically for my accounts receivable customers to pay me in January rather than waiting several months. I kept saying, "Lord, if you want me to continue this business, I really need $23,000—I just need my customers to send me a check for what they owe me."

I can almost hear God chuckling, saying, "That Martha is such a baby Christian. She thinks I don't know exactly what she needs." I know that God has a sense of humor when I look at the way I do things and yet he honors them anyway. Isn't it wonderful how God takes what we ask for and does what is best for us whether we ask for it or not?

Evening, morning and noon I cry out
in distress, and he hears my voice.
—Psalm 55:17

My precious God was listening and answering all along. The invoices I had sent in December began to come back in with those wonderful checks—and all before the end of January! I hadn't made any collection calls and I hadn't sent any registered letters. The checks just seemed to arrive on time. When my bookkeeper added up the amount in our accounts after we had paid salaries, rent, and utilities, there was slightly over $24,000.

I began to weep tears of joy and to say out loud in my book-keeper's office, "Oh, thank you, Lord. Thank you for answering my prayer and for directing me to go on with my sewing ministry. Thank you for this incredible miracle."

Sharing Joy and Blessings through GRACE

The greatest pleasure of my business is sharing the joy of sewing with women all over the world. I am still teaching; how-ever, this time I am making enough money to do the things I would like to do for my family and others. I have funds to make it through the month and some left over to save. I am able to contribute to world missions and to charities here at home. We have educated our children without their having major loans to pay upon graduation. I thank God for all the blessings he has given to me and for showing me how to get to this place in my life through GRACE.

Working with God first in all things, Resilience, Action, Creativity, and Enthusiasm—that's how you find successes and solutions.

I can do everything through him
who gives me strength.
—Philippians 4:13

CHAPTER TWO

The Making of an Entrepreneur

Having my own business was a childhood dream which began with a magazine sale at Scottsboro Elementary School. The publishing company sent a representative to deliver a rousing speech to the students. This gentleman, Mr. Curtis, explained, "You will all have the chance to earn prizes for yourself and for your classroom. You will receive points according to which magazines you sell and, of course, on how much you sell." Each student received a prize book which featured such wonders as a football, a baseball and bat, a basketball, a radio, a comb and brush set, and so forth. The book was colorful and it felt magical in my hands. I thought, *Now I will have my own business*. He shared with us how to go door to door and ask all of our friends and neighbors to buy magazines from us. He shared the technique of "telephone sales" by telling us to call all of our friends that we knew, as well as family members in town and out of town. He asked us to get our parents to sell for us at their places of business. He even told us to take our books to meetings and church. My vision went wild.

> Entrepreneur. One who organizes, manages, and assumes the risks of a business or enterprise. An entrepreneur is an administrator, president, chief, leader, guardian, custodian, overseer, key person.

Mr. Curtis did role playing to show us how to knock on doors, how to open the sales pitch, and how to be prepared by taking pencils, order pads, and a smile. The impact of a lifetime came, however, when he told us what *not* to do when someone opened their door. In a deadpan manner he told us never to say, "You don't want to buy any magazines, do you?"

Wow, what a lesson! For magazine selling or for life, don't ever ask that question.

The other statement Mr. Curtis made that day was, "One of you sitting in this auditorium today will be the top salesman for the whole school. I wonder who it will be?" My heart beat faster and faster as I thought in my little excited brain, *It's going to be me, Mr. Curtis. No one else in this auditorium knows that, but it's going to be me.* (By the way, I did win the magazine sales contest in the fifth grade as well as the sixth. My room got the most candy and I got the most prizes.)

Call it the competitive spirit, call it ambition, call it whatever, I was born with the desire to win and to achieve. Second best wasn't good enough at my house if we could be first. Sloppy wasn't accepted. B's weren't good enough for my mother when she knew I could make A's without much effort.

I started my first business when I was fourteen years old. Living in a small town, there was no dance teacher, so Mama took me to different surrounding cities for dance lessons. Since other people in Scottsboro wanted their children to study dance also, a group of the town mothers asked me if I would start a dance school. Of course, my answer was a resounding, "Yes, I would love to!" Before I could drive a car, my business was thriving. I loved teaching dance and the students seemed to love me. Every Saturday from 8:00 A.M. to 5:00 P.M. I would teach and Mama would play the piano for accompaniment. Since I was a majorette, lots of the kids asked for baton lessons also. So I began to go to the gymnasium of the high school after school and teach baton lessons also. My senior year in high school, I had one hundred dance students per week as well as fifty baton students. I loved every minute of this business experience.

Another wonderful part of the business was that I saved money that completely covered all of my expenses for one and a half years of my college education.

My dream all during high school was to get my degree and move to Huntsville to open a professional children's school which would teach dance, drama, baton, and other related arts. All of my dreams centered around owning my own business. After marriage, children, teaching, attending graduate school, and lots of moving around, I finally achieved my dream of owning my own business when I was thirty-seven years old.

Love What You Do or Do What You Love

The success is to do what you enjoy doing! To love what you do or do what you love. I love teaching sewing and I love doing seminars. We love producing publications that people appreciate and buy. We seem more like a family than a customer/business relationship. In short, I adore my business, my employees, my customers, my business colleagues, and my lifestyle. That is a true blessing from God.

If someone offered me a seven-figure salary to run another company, I would not take it. Now I don't go to work; I go to play. I feel I am in God's will sharing new and exciting sewing skills and teaching other small businesses how to avoid the mistakes I have made. Besides, I do not have the skills to run a business large enough to pay a seven-figure salary. I would have no idea how to manage a business with five hundred employees. I would hate that kind of pressure and would probably be fired before I got to draw even one year's pay.

I think the most important thing for anybody
is to fall in love with what they are doing for a living.
I fell in love with show business when I was eight
years old, and I love it as much today as I did then.
—George Burns (1898-1998),
entertainer, actor

Is It Right for You?

Today you and your hobby are friends. Fun! Entertainment! Wouldn't it be wonderful if you could find a way to make it pay? Pay for itself and bring in a monetary profit as well?

Everything has a price. The price of turning your hobby into an income source is that it is no longer a hobby! It's work. Before you go farther, ask yourself, do I love it that much? If the answer is yes, then this book is for you!

Are You Willing to Pay the Price?

If you want your hobby to bring you income, then it will no longer be a hobby. If you want it to continue to bring you income, you must treat it like a real business: record keeping, taxes, business cards, marketing, liability insurance, etc. Are you willing to pay the price?

I have found that turning sewing into a multi-million-dollar business meant finding aspects of "business" that were as much fun as my hobby. Often this took some creative thinking on my part, as it will on yours.

That, of course is what this book is about: dealing with the mundane aspects of business and searching for ways to make it easier, and more fun.

Doing what you are passionate about thirteen hours a day is fulfilling, but it is also consuming. If I had it to do over again, I would do exactly the same as I have already done (without some of the mistakes, of course). For me the price was well worth the purchase. Only you can answer this question in your own situation in life.

Do You Have What It Takes?

In my planning stage I loved imagining that if I had my own business, I could do anything I wanted to at any time I deemed necessary! I wouldn't have to go to another town to work, and would be close to my five children, ages fifteen, fourteen, fourteen, thirteen, and four. I would have all the time

I needed to be a mother and attend plays, teacher's conferences, and other events. I would have time to take my children to their physician's appointments, orthodontist's appointments, and other appointments. I could again "do" lovely little dinner parties for eight.

Ah well, so much for the fantasy.

You will not become an entrepreneur to work less—you will work more, much more. The difference will be you are doing what you love!

Later we will discuss ways to keep your family loved and secure, a happy part of your new lifestyle.

Do you have what it takes? Ask yourself these questions:

1. Do I spend my free time looking for tasks to do?
2. Do I plunge right in when something needs to be done and disdain the need to talk things over with friends before I make a decision?
3. Do I enjoy physical and emotional exhaustion?
4. Do I enjoy chaos?
5. Do I love to do ten things at once?
6. Am I organized?
7. Can I handle stress?
8. Do I have a competitive spirit?
9. Am I prepared to make financial sacrifices for several years or more?
10. Do I have the skills/background?
11. Do I know how to sell my product?
12. Do I love my product?
13. Am I a great communicator and generally find people attracted to me?
14. Do I enjoy (or tolerate) planning ahead—a week, a month, a year?
15. Have I always been considered a leader?
16. Do I have a *burning* desire to be my own boss?
17. Do I think I can't live much longer if I don't start my own business?

18. Am I disciplined in finishing tasks?
19. Am I optimistic? Do I think positively and consider problems challenges rather than problems?
20. Am I a confident person?
21. Can I stand risk-taking?
22. Can I stand the thought of bookkeeping, raising money, juggling cash flow?
23. Do workers like to work with and for me?
24. Do I really like working with people and talking with people?
25. Am I willing to travel excessively if necessary?
26. Am I willing to take classes to learn accounting and computer skills if necessary?
27. Do I really like to sell?
28. Have I had success in the past in selling?
29. Do I have enough money to pay the bills for a long period of time?
30. Am I willing to use my savings to get this venture off the ground?
31. Is my spouse willing to do without my salary to help me get this business off the ground?
32. Am I willing to work without a paycheck for weeks, months, maybe years?
33. Am I willing to give up my weekends?
34. Is my spouse supportive of this venture?
35. Are my children and spouse willing to help me do whatever is necessary as far as helping with business chores, household chores, and other things?

If you answered yes to at least twenty-five of these questions, you have what it takes to turn your hobby to profit. You have what it takes to be an entrepreneur.

Do You Know Enough?

Of course before you find ways to make your hobby pay, you must become somewhat of an expert. I say *somewhat* because the people who make real money from their hobbies are rarely the leading experts. The ones who make money use their passion, drive, and ambition; rarely do they succeed because of their expertise.

A constant study of your subject will not only make you more of an expert, and therefore more in demand, but it will also show you new ways to profit. Warren Ogren was an amateur beekeeper whose hobby has blossomed into a multi-million-dollar business. Ogren, a "mad scientist" type who holds several patents on his various inventions, was reading a trade journal for beekeepers when he came across an ad seeking to buy a substance called Propolis for an astounding $90 per pound. Propolis, the dark, hard, sticky stuff honeybees use to seal and sterilize their hives, was regarded as a useless byproduct by most North American beekeepers. After some research, however, Ogren discovered that Propolis has distinct antibacterial, antifungal, and antiviral properties, and is highly prized as a natural medicine, especially in Europe and Asia. So he established a network for gathering bulk Propolis (it's scraped out of the insides of beehives once a year) from beekeepers all over the country. Ogren's daughter, Linda Graham, quit her job as an X-ray technician to join, and later buy, her father's company. Today, Beehive Botanicals does business in thirty countries, is the largest dealer in Propolis in North America, and markets a full line of skin care, personal care, and dietary supplement products—all of which use the gifts of the honeybee as the central ingredient. Yearly sales are just under $3 million.

Certainly, your first step is to become good at your hobby and to always continue in the learning process. How can you become an expert? Here are a few places to look for information:

- check your local and county libraries
- visit used bookstores
- keep your own reference materials and software
- subscribe to magazines and newsletters
- join associations

- join users groups
- go to seminars and lectures regularly
- offer to assist other speakers and experts in your field
- subscribe to on-line information providers, newsgroups, and forums
- check the Internet Reference
- attend classes through your local colleges, adult education programs, or parks and recreation departments

I Can't Because . . .

Once you know your hobby fairly well, I suggest you let go of all you have learned about why you can't make money with it. Many people come to me and say, "Martha! I'm ready! I want to start earning income with _____. Help me with ideas of how to do it!"

"Wonderful! Have you thought about giving lessons?" From the looks on their faces I can see that won't do. "How about trade shows? No?"

"Martha you don't understand, I can't because . . . "

"I can't because . . ." How sad. They actually know too much—too many reasons they can't succeed. The truth is, there are thousands of reasons they can. However, their preconceptions get in their way. If you are ready to gear your mind toward making money with your hobby, empty your mind first. Allow the wonder of the hundreds of possibilities available to you to flow in. Start over as a beginner.

If your mind is empty, it is always ready for anything; it is open to everything. In the beginner's mind there are many possibilities, but in the expert's there are few.
—Shunryu Suzuki, founder of
Suzuki violin teaching method

Better to Try and Fail . . .

My retail store taught me a lot about what sells and what doesn't. It gave me many experiences to use in my business seminars with other retailers. I tried lots of things that didn't work, but I have become stronger from my mistakes and have become a better consultant by having lived through some whoppers. It is my pleasure to help others not make those mistakes.

Even though I had a successful career as a teacher, at age thirty-seven the words of the poets, philosophers, and prophets that I had been teaching to others illuminated a path in my life. I realized I would rather try and fail than never to try at all. I had the overwhelming feeling that if I didn't try *now*, I would wake up at age sixty-five and tell myself, "What if I had tried that business?" Would I die with my music unsung?

"Far better it is to dare mighty things,
to win glorious triumphs,
even though checkered by failure,
than to take rank with those poor spirits
who neither enjoy much nor suffer much.
Because they live in the gray twilight that knows not
victory nor defeat."
—Teddy Roosevelt,
Former U.S. President,
speech before the Hamilton Club
(Chicago, April 10, 1899)

CHAPTER THREE

Finding the Right Ideas for You

In this section we will help you think of ideas for profit making and show you how to decide if your hobby is the kind that can be a commercial success, how to start thinking of ideas for your hobby business, and how to test your hobby for possible areas of profitability.

There are thousands of ways to make your hobby pay. Please do not be limited by the many ideas we will show you in this section. Use these ideas as a springboard to help you create even more ways to earn income.

Adversity Introduces You to Yourself and to Great Ideas

Inspiration comes in many ways. Often ideas on how to make your hobby pay will come out of a great deal of pain. I feel God is always talking to me, offering me advice, giving me ideas. Sometimes I get busy and forget to pay attention. I think these painful lessons are God's way of getting my attention when I get caught up with myself.

Traditionally in the South, where I have spent most of my life, when someone is selling you something they are very nice and polite while you make your decisions and write them a check. We like to think of ourselves as famous for our Southern hospitality. I just assumed the rest of the world did things like we all do down here in Huntsville. . . .

. . . and then I went on my first trip to the big city to buy supplies for my new store.

"Hurry!" "Make up your mind!" "Come on, come on, COME ON!" The sellers were too busy to help me and to encourage me about my choices. It would be the understatement of the century to grace it by calling it bad salesmanship; they had no salesmanship at all. They practically slammed the doors behind our backs after we had written our checks. I was in tears after leaving one place. I had spent my life savings and these individuals had been truly rude to me.

I have heard it said that "adversity introduces a man to himself." You often find the best ideas in the worst situations. As Joe and I flew home from that nightmare experience, we began to ask each other, "I wonder if there is a market for those products to be brought in by someone else who knows how to treat customers and how to say 'thank you for your business'?" It didn't take a great leap of our imaginations to decide that there certainly must be some normal people out there who would appreciate "nice."

Joe began making contacts with his dental friends in France and Switzerland to ask them to find where these laces and embroideries were manufactured. Before long our dental friends sent us the names of lace and fabric companies. They had even contacted these companies personally for us to tell them that we were coming. They opened the doors for us to purchase goods.

We purchased inventory to import and made our plans for selling it. We knew of one convention and one trade show, so we purchased booths. At first we simply posted samples on boards and took orders. For the next show we got really fancy and made photocopies of the laces and samples of the batiste and embroideries. Wow! Our first catalog.

We built an empire—one business at a time: first the retail store, Martha Pullen's heirloom shop; then Martha Pullen Co., Wholesale Import Division. Today we have added two magazines and a television show. It really began because of that painful day with those rude clerks far away from Huntsville.

Gail Lang is a classic example of something wonderful being created from an adverse situation. She refers to herself as simply "a mother of four, housewife, and community volunteer. No title, no job, no degrees, no college, just a hard working dedicated mother, wife and citizen." Then she began having difficulties with allergies. The problem became so severe that for almost a year she found herself home alone, all of her activities ground to a halt, with little contact other than her family and her hobby, her computer. The illness took away the community involvement she loved, but the computer allowed her to replace that with a virtual world. Over time, while her immune system was healing, she found the Internet. Here was a world she could be part of with no fear of illness or death. She found friends she could talk to and share with and have no fear of physical harm. For many months the Net helped her keep her sanity and find something to focus on. Together with her new Internet friends she turned her hobby into her own business on the Internet.

Her immune system became rejuvenated from the time alone, and the business became a profitable adventure branching out into two unique divisions providing a multitude of Internet services to the world. "I think there are several reasons for my success," says Gail. "Two more important of course being my determination and positive attitude. These combined with base skills such as the ability to adapt, ability to work with others, ability to plan and structure, and a true talent for that which I do, all combine to give me the ability to succeed."

The English word *crisis* is translated by the Chinese with two little characters; one means "danger," the other "opportunity." When Laura's husband died she tried with difficulty to run his gas station by herself. Adversity can give you some wonderful ideas. She wasn't too good at running a gas station, but she knew how to cook great potato chips. She gave her gasoline customers a free sample, then sold them sackfuls in brown paper bags. She invented sealed sacks that would keep her potato chips fresh: Laura folded waxed paper and sealed it with a hot iron on her ironing board.

Then Laura went out to call on grocery stores armed with samples for them to taste and her new sacks of potato chips for them to buy. She always wore a hat and a big smile. Her company became one of the largest in the West—"Laura Scudders."

Is there adversity in your life that has prompted you to pick up this book? In prayer, ask for wisdom to allow the situation to introduce you to yourself and to better understand your dreams. You often find the best ideas in the worst situations. Always remember that God is sovereign and he is in control.

Character cannot be developed in ease and quiet.
Only through experience of trial and suffering can the
soul be strengthened, vision cleared, ambition
inspired, and success achieved.
—Helen Keller (1880–1968),
U.S. blind/deaf author, lecturer

Can Your Hobby Be a Commercial Success?

Some hobbies will never be marketable. One person I know collects one species of rare Tibetan butterflies. Let's take a brief reality check: The market for the advanced studies of Tibetan butterflies is very limited.

To discover what will be a commercial success, follow the age-old business adage: Find a need and fill it.

Smocking was enjoying a revival right after my daughter, Joanna, was born. Supplies were hard to find and technique books were almost nonexistent. Having a daughter after four sons was one of the most exciting things that had ever happened in my life. Once I discovered smocking and French sewing, I began the desperate search for a pleating machine, patterns, laces, batiste, and other needed items for my hobby. Traveling over two hours to a tiny shop with limited supplies was inconvenient, to say the least. The need was clear. There was no smocking shop in Huntsville; a number of my friends were in the same situation of having to scrounge around for materials. I filled that need by opening a smocking shop.

Choosing Your Field

You must be careful when you are exploring options under the "find a need and fill it" system. It is easy for those of us with a passion for a hobby to assume "Of course there is a need there!" simply because *you* have a need.

I remember watching the movie *The Making of an American Quilt*. The themes eloquently state how we make choices. It occurred to me that day that the choices in business are very similar to choices in one's life in other areas.

Take, for example, choosing between a lover and a friend for a life partner. Eventually the heroine in the movie chooses her friend over the gorgeous lover. In the business world choosing a project which is friendly rather than glamorous is much safer and usually more lucrative. There is a huge difference between being a risk taker and being blinded by the glamour of a situation. Once again, I am speaking from experience!

Once in my business life, I chose a glamorous project. My daughter, Joanna, loved competing in pageants. She especially enjoyed the talent and speech competitions. I was thrilled to share my own lifelong love of dancing with my daughter, as well as make her beautiful evening gowns. But, you know me, gotta turn all my hobbies into profit! I began a magazine, *Pageants and Talent*, which focused on dancers, pageant winners, costumes, and evening wear. Just one little problem: I hadn't researched to see if my consumers were interested in this type of magazine.

The costumes in *Pageants and Talent* were very designer-styled and either intricate to make or expensive to hire someone else to make. The reality of the dance world is that costumes come from houses in New York and retail for about $50. Having someone make one of the wonderful costumes we suggested would cost them at least $500. Just because I loved dance didn't mean that other mothers of dancers would want to buy or make expensive costumes and gowns, when great costumes are available so easily. I decided to close down this venture and just enjoy my daughter, dance, pageants, and speech contests.

That closed a very expensive chapter in my business life—the perusing of the glamorous rather than the friendly opportunities.

To Get You Started

Many of us start off knowing we love our hobbies. But we are not sure how we can profit from them, nor what our personal strengths are. To find your own personal strengths, ask yourself these questions:

- What do you like to do with your time?
- What technical skills have you learned or developed?
- What do others say you are good at doing?
- How much time do you have to run a business?
- What do you love most about doing your hobby? The skill? The people?

For instance, if what you really like about your stamp collecting hobby is the people you get to socialize with, and what everyone says you do well is make cookies, then sell cookies at the gatherings of your stamp collecting group! Take orders, get business cards, set up a little cookie stand out of the back of your car, rent a booth, whatever it takes. Or perhaps what you really love is creating the craft of your hobby, in which case you would want to consider selling or teaching. Find something associated with your hobby from which you can make a profit.

Test Your Hobby for Profitability

I wish I could have "tested" some of the great possibilities I tried. To see if your hobby is the sort that you could turn into a business, ask yourself this series of questions:

- Market Size: Is there an abundance of people who enjoy this same interest? Is there a way you can do a test of the market? Or get the results from others who have done market tests?

- Market Interest: Do you think others would enjoy this hobby if they knew about it? Is it interesting to new people?
- Market Saturation: Are there lots of outlets already available for purchase of hobby materials? Are there plenty of shops offering classes in your hobby area?
- Future Innovation: Can you think of new products you might develop which you might sell in your business? If your business is sailing, can you write books about sailing or start a sailing magazine? Can you import goods for Americans that are already enjoyed by people in other countries?
- Uniqueness: Is your hobby fresh enough that everybody isn't already doing it and getting tired of it? Are there just a few porcelain doll makers in your community?
- Possibilities for Creative Expansion: Does your hobby have new avenues after people get tired of the current ones?

The next step is to determine what niche your business will fill. The following questions will help guide you:

- Is your idea practical, and will it fill a need?
- What is your competition?
- What is your advantage over existing businesses?
- Can you deliver a higher/better quality service?
- Can you create a demand for your business?

Passions with Integrity, Pride, and Honor

I don't have much patience with people who talk a great deal about integrity and honor. I agree with Ralph Waldo Emerson when he said, "The louder he talked of his honor, the faster we counted our spoons!"[1]

As you explore your own dreams, ask yourself this: "When the journey is over, will the people who matter most look at me and say, 'Well done!'?" Which of the many choices—thirty years from now—will make you stand a bit taller? I like to believe that the books and magazines we write will be treasured a hundred years from now. For me, the most satisfying part of the business is being able to bring spiritual encouragement to readers of our magazines in the "Dear Friends" page of *Sew Beautiful.*

> *Never undertake anything for which you wouldn't*
> *have the courage to ask the blessings of heaven.*
> —G. C. Lichtenberg (1742–99),
> German physicist, philosopher

CHAPTER FOUR

Ways to Make a Hobby Pay

So, you go to that street fair and notice that many of the people there get thirsty . . . sell drinks!

You give dance lessons and hear people complaining that they can't find the right shoes . . . take orders!

You hear the people at dog shows say they just can't find those lovely colors anywhere for the special dog beds . . . find a manufacturer and sell them yourself!

While off-roading on your bike, you notice people love to eat a certain type of food . . . bring it and sell it!

Listen to the people around you. Hear what they are complaining about. Mr. Heinz saw his mother cry while grating fresh horseradish for his father. (Horseradish is much worse than onions.) He got the idea of grating horseradish by machine. That product started his 57 varieties.

Most of our hobbies begin by just being great fun, if rather expensive. Margina Dennis's hobby was fashion, everything from shopping to make-up application. This hobby became costly because of the time it required and the courses she took in make-up application, figure analysis, image consulting, color theory, and public speaking. Then she began to generate income by working as a freelance make-up artist and by working with companies, groups, and individuals as an image and communication consultant. Today she generates a minimum of $2,000 a month in revenue working part-time. "I feel I have been successful because I'm really enjoying what I'm doing and I'm helping others. I receive some of the most heartwarming letters from clients that feel I have helped them to change their lives."

You may start with one idea and then learn it has many other possibilities as you go along, as did Lou Kennedy. Lou's joy was home entertaining. During the ten years that her husband was in the Army, Lou enjoyed preparing her favorite Louisiana Creole and Cajun dishes and entertaining military friends as they moved across the United States and Okinawa. She continued to entertain at home when they settled in Corpus Christi, Texas. In 1987, Lou was asked to conduct a workshop for teenagers on dining skills and social graces. It was so successful that she immediately created her own training company for adults and is now a successful executive coach specializing in business and social etiquette, professional image, and communication skills. Lou has addressed thousands of professionals over the years as she travels across the United States and Canada conducting workshops and consulting. She has written two business etiquette books using the traditional etiquette rules of the past and incorporating current trends for the new millennium. One fun offshoot of her hobby led to others.

Here are many ways you can make your hobby pay:

- take custom orders
- give home parties
- sell wholesale to retail and consignment stores
- teach classes and lessons (in homes and stores)
- be a spokesperson or sponsor
- be a consultant
- write educational articles
- sell at craft shows and street fairs
- sell at trade shows
- host celebrity events to promote your business
- create your own catalog and sell to others
- create additional products and services using your hobby (books, tapes, manuals, etc.)
- sell internationally
- create your own retail store

Take Custom Orders

Many hobby-driven businesses have started with someone making a beautiful object—a painted box, a stuffed animal, a portrait of a child, a sketch of a house turned into a note card, a creative birthday cake, a doll dress, a porcelain doll, a piece of furniture, a dried flower arrangement, a piece of jewelry, or anything else—and having others ask if they could buy one just like it. I call this the custom-order business.

In the heirloom sewing business, several seamstresses really customize the order and have the potential customers come in for an interview about their special order. These seamstresses usually have a picture portfolio of dresses that they have made in the past.

Some of these seamstresses charge up to $1,500 for a dress. I know of one woman who charged $10,000 for a christening dress that had over one thousand hours of embroidery. Perhaps you think the world is a little crazy when people pay $1,500 for a child's dress for a portrait. Do you know what many portrait artists charge for painting an oil portrait? Twenty-five thousand dollars isn't uncommon and even an excellent portrait studio many times charges over $1,000 for a photograph beautifully done.

"Word of mouth" is the main way the custom-order business is born and advanced. You may find word of mouth spreads the message to so many people that you have more business than you want. I know some doll makers who only use word of mouth. They are so well known that customers wait in line for years for one of their dolls. On the other hand, most of us work like crazy to promote our business!

Give Home Parties

A home party, which is often called a trunk showing, will be one of the first things you do to sell your products. Make several things and be prepared to take orders. Many financial empires have been built on the concept of home parties—Mary Kay, Princess House, Tupperware, House of Lloyds, Amway.

Why shouldn't your's? You could use the same strategy for almost any hobby-based business.

Choose a hostess and make her responsible for getting a certain number of people together for the event. Have your goods ready to take custom orders if yours is a custom-order business. Have a selection; don't take orders for just anything anyone dreams of. Have specific samples of your selections and be prepared to give a delivery date. Most companies have a hostess discount or gift, sometimes a percentage of the total sales.

If you are selling supplies for a hobby, then have your goods present. You can sell your goods via take-home or "order and deliver." You will have greater sales if they can see and touch the product for spur-of-the-moment purchasing. On the other hand, low inventory is one of the best assets of a business and is much easier to deal with. So carefully examine what you want to have on hand.

Sell Wholesale to Retail and Consignment Stores

Another way to get custom orders and sales of any type is to take your goods or services to someone else's shop for resale. The shop can take the orders for you, buy and resell your product, or sell them on consignment. If your product is new to a store, they might be hesitant to buy it from you. If so, ask them to try it on consignment. Selling goods on consignment means the shop owner has them with the provision that payment is made only on completed sales and that unsold items may be returned to you.

Remember, you are selling to them wholesale which, for most places, is one-half of the normal retail price. This might seem like a huge cut in your profit. However, the store is paying for the overhead: phones, employees, advertising, building rent. Fifty percent is actually a small price to pay for the huge reduction in your expenses and risk. Make sure to keep careful records of where you have sent your goods on consignment. Check back periodically to see how they are doing and to offer advice.

Finding the appropriate stores that might want to sell your product is not difficult. If your hobby involves creation of a product (crafts, books, etc.), find places that sell similar or complimentary products. If your product is good for people recovering in a hospital, go to the hospital gift stores, florist shops, pharmacies that carry gift items, etc. If you are making a snack item, just open your mind to places where people need to wait around: car washes, gas stations, Little League games. The world is full of opportunities.

Don't expect the store to do all the promotions. Estee Lauder began her business by creating her makeup products in her kitchen. She would then go into the department stores and help them in every way she could to promote her product over her competition's. She was one of the first to push the "gift with purchase." She gave lectures on makeup to customers and helped the salespeople understand her products.

Teach Classes and Lessons

Teaching—giving classes, seminars, and lessons—is one of the most obvious ways to increase your income (by charging for the lessons) and is a brilliant marketing tool for your product or service. Many huge companies were started this way. We have dedicated an entire section to this in chapter 11, "Publications, Classes, and Events." Teach lessons at your local shop, a local junior college, a community education program, or at your home or church.

Many times excellent lesson plans can be turned into a how-to book with very little editing. My dear friend Mildred Turner began teaching sewing at a local junior college. She later opened a smocking shop in Asheville, North Carolina. When she came to my school of art fashion in Huntsville, she brought her lesson plans and her instruction sheets. I looked at those plans and said, "Mildred, you have at least three heirloom sewing books already written. When are you going to have them ready for sale?" In a short time she had the first book ready.

You might even become a professional speaker through your hobby. "Doc" Blakely was a college professor, teaching animal husbandry at Wharton County Junior College. His hobby was speaking, telling jokes, and entertaining at banquets for grins and a free meal. This gradually led to people giving him small honorariums or telling him they had a budget of so many dollars. Soon he discovered he was making more money off his hobby than his job, so he quit and went full-time. "I was lucky enough to come along at the right time when the industry of speaking was in its infancy, my humor was unique, my timing and stage presence was superior to most of the competition at the time and I was a bargain compared to the established speakers of that day. From then on it was continuing education and careful risk taking." (For more on this, see *Speak and Grow Rich* by Dottie and Lilly Walters, Prentice-Hall Simon Schuster.)

Teaching Lessons at Home

You can offer private lessons or group classes in your home or theirs. No one is going to complain about private lessons, but group lessons may bring complaints from your neighbors if you don't have plenty of room. Many zoning laws don't allow group teaching in a home. In areas where zoning prohibits home-based businesses, groups are protesting and trying to change the laws. It is better to find out the zoning laws before you begin your planning than to have a neighbor call the zoning people after you have set up your classes.

You must have a space designated for the lessons. Think about what you intend to teach. For a sewing class, a dining room table is good if you have enough plugs for the sewing machines. What kind of space would lessons for your group require?

Tips for At-Home Teaching Professionalism

This is not a social group that has come to your home. Your must treat it with the professionalism required for any business venture.

- Have a list of all requirements: start times, rules, needed materials, safety tips, important phone numbers, anything they might need to know.
- Prepare all of your supplies and the location before your students arrive.
- Take care of possible disturbances: Turn on the answering machine, put a "do not disturb" sign on your front and back doors, have all children out of the way and taken care of, or trained to be assistants.
- Start class promptly on time. Do not penalize the prompt people by waiting for the latecomers.
- Charge students in advance for a block of lessons, with no refunds if they don't show.
- Some students will want to stay long after the lesson is over. In preliminary information state when the class will begin and end and the rates for which you are available for private consulting after the class time is up. This informs students that your time is not theirs for free and that they will be expected to leave when the class is over. This is much more professional, and certainly less rude, than if you just try to run them off. Professionals charge a client for every minute over the hour that was paid for; you should do the same.
- Create "release forms" and have students sign them. These are not going to stop you from getting sued, but they are some help. Talk to your attorney.
- Don't wait until someone falls down in your living room to find out that your insurance policy doesn't cover business guests in your home. Check your homeowner's policy; double check with your agent.

In-Store Teaching

Teaching in stores that already have a clientele of possible customers can be an ideal situation. Just ask yourself, "Where do I purchase the supplies needed to do my hobby? Where do other enthusiasts of my hobby go to shop?" Approach these places of business about the possibility of your offering a class there. It will increase their sales, and you gain income from the classes and a bigger base of possible sales for your product or service. For instance, if your hobby is square dancing, where do you buy the costumes? If your hobby is gardening, where is the best place to buy plants?

Share-the-Gate Classes

There are many groups that offer "share-the-gate" classes. In a share-the-gate, you supply the program. The sponsor provides the hall, refreshment breaks, advertising, their list of prospects, postage, printing, and sometimes travel expenses. Usually the sponsor organization sells all of the tickets. Often, you will be allowed to sell products at the back of the room. The usual arrangement is a fifty-fifty split of the gate, although different organizations work at various percentage levels.

The possibilities are endless! Look at any business or association that might want to increase their visibility. Here is a list to start with in your own community, but do not let this list limit you. Open your mind and see what other ideas come to you!

- colleges
- churches
- PTAs
- parks and recreation departments
- school booster clubs
- hospitals
- Chambers of Commerce
- service clubs (Rotary, Kiwanis, Lions, etc.)
- on-line seminar classes
- associations
- Urban Independent Adult Education seminar companies

To sell your classes to any of these, you must have appropriate lesson plans and a flyer on what your program will cover. Have a current resumé with references. If you have never taught anything, then use personal references. Then simply make an appointment to see the director. They are eager for good programs. You can organize a traveling school and store.

Tips on Professionalism in Share-the-Gate Classes

- Check ahead about supplies which will be needed, including electrical outlets, tables, chairs, easels, chalkboards, etc.
- Check about liability insurance for any teacher in the event of an accident.
- Find out if you can sell materials on the premises to your students, and how students get supplies in general.
- Check out the room and make plans with the administration about students who will need to bring their own equipment such as sewing machines, cameras, or other types of things.

Spokespersons and Sponsors

You have seen athletes who are spokespersons for national firms. Many companies often look for experts to be spokespersons for their products, services, or public image. The American Floral Service hires many florists whom they train to speak on a variety of subjects such as floral arrangements, the history and meaning of flowers, appropriate flowers to deliver a message, etc. They sponsor these presenters to speak at conventions and meetings of all kinds where AFS clients and potential clients are gathered. The Canon Home Copier company hired Paul and Sarah Edwards, speakers and experts in the area of home businesses, to speak on television across the nation to promote Canon's products. This proved to be a perfect tie-in with the couple's famous series of books on working from home.

Consulting

The best way to become a successful consultant is to run a successful business—with a high profile.

The next time someone says, "Will you help me with . . .," very nicely say, "Of course! I'll just fax you my consulting rate sheet." When someone says, "May I have a few minutes of your time?" reply with, "I wish I could, but I must go prepare for my students who have paid for my consulting time. Would you like to schedule some time?" Your time and expertise are worth something! Don't be afraid to value it.

Consider calling yourself a "personal coach" or a "personal trainer" as a form of consulting. Create a system whereby you will help your customers obtain their goals in regards to your area of expertise. For a fee they might call in once a week for a half-hour session with you. Most coaches charge around $300 per month for this service. Doing it via phone and/or E-mail will greatly reduce your costs and time.

Write Educational Articles

How many hours have you spent studying your hobby? Well, you are an expert! As an expert you can also become in demand as a paid journalist. Many hobbyists earn a substantial amount from the articles they produce for various publications. Writing articles is a fantastic passive method of marketing.

Craft Shows and Street Fairs

There are literally thousands of craft shows and street fairs around the USA. Normally they advertise in your local newspaper. Ask others who sell at or create these shows which catalog and magazines they advertise in. For instance, in Southern California there are many, including *The Crafts Fair Guide*, published in Mill Valley, which lists about one thousand fairs held in California parks, schools, homes, and businesses.

Trade Shows

A trade show is a gathering of exhibitors who sell, or showcase, their products to attendees. Exhibitors usually have their products in booths of varying types. Trade shows can be a terrific source of sales of your product or service if you target the right audience. If you have a capability to produce "enough" of your product, you might want to take your product to a major merchandise mart and show it to some of the showrooms. Remember that you are now selling to people who will be selling wholesale to stores. Stores have to put a double markup on it before taking it to the customers. The representatives will need a cut, probably 10 to 15 percent in order to handle the orders for their customers. Once you start selling below wholesale cost, your profit fizzles. But if your price can be high enough, then this might be a good way to get a custom-order business.

Co-Op with Others for Trade Show Sales

Buying your own booth at a trade show can be expensive. Look for several others with related, yet noncompeting, products and/or services. If you combine your funds and time, the costs becomes much easier to bear. Also, you can take turns working in the booth.

Become a Representative for Related Products

Many companies need to hire people to work trade shows and present their product to the community. Look at the supplies you are currently using and like best. Contact these companies about being a representative for them.

Don't give up if they say no—keep trying every few months. Enthusiasm and perseverance are valuable traits that they will admire.

Host Your Own Trade Show, Craft Show, or Street Fair

There is an amazing amount of money to be made in creating your own event. The trick is to have an event where you are sure you will have an audience. One way to insure an audience is to hire a celebrity to speak at the event. Another is to find a group that already has a crowd—churches, schools, shopping centers, etc.—and offer to host an event for them. Your event will bring them more traffic; their traffic will buy from your vendors!

I created fashion show events to help sales. The garments on warm human beings speak for themselves. I use my teaching methods to tell a little about how they were made. We then sell our products at the back of the room.

Host Celebrity Events to Promote Your Business

A celebrity event is usually a seminar, or speech, given by a celebrity in your field. Having a celebrity event associated with you and your business can put you on the fast track to success. It will also bring:

- energy to your business
- excitement to your customers and staff
- new customers
- new class ideas
- sales, both at the event and afterwards
- entertainment (show business) to your business image
- press interest

I remember when Art Linkletter was the "big name" traveling in retirement seminars, health seminars, etc. He posed for pictures for all the people who underwrote the event. My husband, a dentist, was one of the sponsors. It was attended by thousands of people and meant a huge increase for his business. This type of event can be applied to many different types of businesses.

Create Your Own Catalog

Today even the cheapest computer can create simple catalogs that are really very nice for the small business. Keep a database of potential clients. Catalogs should be updated and mailed to your potential client base at least twice a year, monthly if your budget can afford it.

Always include a catalog in every order you sell!

The Web

Include your entire catalog on the Web. It is not that expensive and is becoming easier to access every day. If your hobby is related to technology in any way, then creating your own Web site is a must. Most of your potential clientele most likely have Internet access and will look there first.

Sell through Other Catalogs and Direct Mail

There are literally thousands of catalogs that sell through the mail directly to the consumer. They are always looking for products to sell, and why shouldn't yours be one of them?

An important fringe benefit of catalog sales is that your name and products are publicized free. You also gain a prospect for future sales from the sale of the product.

Every time you see a catalog, look for products that might be a compliment to yours. Seek publications whose audiences have a keen interest in what you have to offer. Call and ask for the person who purchases their products. Ask how those other products have done for them in sales. If they have done well, they will be looking for new products.

Catalog companies purchase your product at wholesale and resell it at the retail price. They will usually make one of several types of arrangements with you.

Larger catalog companies will purchase your product in bulk, warehouse it themselves, and resell it at the retail price.

Purchases may be small, only five to ten items, or huge orders into the thousands. It all depends on the popularity of your products and the size of the readership of the catalog.

Purchase your products via drop-ship. The term *drop-ship* means that your products are advertised in someone else's catalog, magazine, or direct mailing piece. The catalog "drops" the order in the mail to you, and you "ship" it, rather than the company warehousing products themselves. Here's how it works. The producer of the catalog or magazine pays for the advertising. They sell your product at full retail, plus a shipping fee. They keep 50 percent (usually) of the retail price and send you (1) the balance, (2) the shipping fee, and (3) a label with the name and address of the buyer. You fill the order.

Sell you space in their catalog. Catalogs often are overwhelmed with products, so they must say no to some requests. However, many will sell you space in their catalogs or in their "special offer" packages. Check other catalogs with products that are appropriate to your target market. If they won't carry your products any other way, consider buying space.

Catalog sales work well if you can create your products in high enough quantities to get the wholesale cost down. For example: You sell your item wholesale for $44.75. The retail price is $89.50. The catalog company makes the sale and keeps $44.75. If the item only cost you $25 to produce, then you make a nice profit.

Create Additional Products and Services

People buy expertise. You are an expert! Don't worry that there are many people with greater experience than you; there are also many with less who are hungry for the knowledge you have gathered. Find ways of helping them get that knowledge. You can create books, booklets, videos, audio albums, workbooks, CD ROMs, training materials, reports, calendars, posters, magazine articles, posters, screen savers, software programs, T-shirts, hats, and even toys based on your expertise. Sales of products can do more than boost your level of income. Creating excellent products also adds credibility and prestige to your power position as an expert.

Dan Poynter was taking finals in law school when a friend suggested a parachute jump. He went out to make one jump and fell in love with freefall flying. Soon he was spending a great deal of income and time on his new passion. So he found a way to turn his passion center into a profit center. "The parachute business was much more interesting than law. Though law was fascinating and the course of study very useful, I became a parachute designer. I would design them Monday through Friday and jump them on the weekends. Soon I began writing for a skydiving magazine. Then I took the collected info, did more research, and published a book. The book established my credibility in the field. I was elected to the board of the U.S. Parachute association and rose to Chairman of the Board. Today, I have written over seventy-five books. Writing and publishing are my business." Dan feels that "your book is the foundation of your business; all else is built on top of it. Your book provides more credibility than anything else you can do."

Selling Internationally

To help American businesses export their products, the government offers many services at little or no cost. The Trade Information Center (1-800-872-8723) is a "one-stop" source for finding out about all of the federal government's export programs. They can provide you with information on getting started, locating foreign markets, financing, and other topics. Their free booklet entitled *Export Programs: A Business Directory of U.S. Government Resources* lists the names and numbers of contacts within various government agencies.

Create Your Own Retail Store

Many hobbyists dream of the day they can start their own store. Of course, this takes the most amount of risk and work on your part. But someday you might be ready, as I was, to take the risk and go forth.

To find the information needed to open your own store, carefully go over Part 2: The Plan. There we have many resources for new business owners, like the Small Business Administration.

Also consider opening a store with someone else who has related products. There is an organ store in Lilly's hometown. An enterprising music hobbyist rents out a back corner and sells sheet music. A win-win for everyone. Customers buying organs have easy access to all kinds of music. The organ store owner gets more traffic into his store and an add-on service to his buyers. The sheet music store owner gets the benefit of all customers coming in to buy organs and a greatly reduced rent over what he normally would have paid.

There are also many small "mall" stores that specialize in things like antiques or crafts. Each vendor has a small space. The most common area I have seen in this style of store is a twelve-by-twelve-foot space. You then create your own store in this area. Your rent includes the services of a cashier in the front of the store so you rarely need to be there.

Selling Products from Your Home

Even if your zoning laws do not allow a home retail business of this type, you might be able to have samples and take orders from home before or right after classes that you teach in your home. You can arrange with your suppliers to ship the product directly to your customers. Some very famous people brought their hobby to profit by starting in their own homes: Henry Ford started in his garage; Laura Scudders began by making potato chips in her kitchen; and Mrs. Knotts started her jams, and Estee Lauder her cosmetics, all from home.

If you teach for someone else in their store, be very careful of how you sell products outside of their influence. You must be totally loyal and supportive of all the store sells. Once a fabric store owner said to me, "Martha, I have a wonderful smocking teacher in my store; however, we are not selling any smocking machines at all. Is that the usual case?" Upon further investigation, the owner found that the teacher told the students, "Call me and I will order your smocking machine cheaper than the ones here." She not only lost her job; the shop owner carefully called the other retail fabric businesses in town to warn them about this teacher who sold under the table. This teacher would have done better to renegotiate her contract with the store to include a commission for her on each machine sold.

You can take your trunk of goods out to teach if you teach for an organization that does not do retail and if you have cleared the selling of product with them first. You must not sell "from your trunk" if you are teaching in a store that sells the same products.

Be sure if you have cleared any sales that you collect the proper taxes and pay them. Do not ever think you can get away without paying your taxes or reporting your sales. This is illegal and very dangerous. The IRS can audit your goods and your sales any time it wishes. You must be accountable for all sales and goods that have been sold.

Traveling Retail Store

Create a store from which your fellow hobbyists can buy what they need. You can sell right out of your car or van or buy booth space at your hobby events. This is a "traveling retail store." In addition to what you have made for your hobby, "other related items" are great attractions for people to see.

Where to Look for Professional Help in Turning Your Hobby to Profit

I had many mentors who helped me greatly along the way. I was good at my craft of sewing, but turning it to profit required lots of wonderful people to assist me. Carole Pichney did the same: "I have consulted with top experts on marketing, such as Dottie Walters, and her advice has been invaluable. Since implementing her suggestions, my career has taken off even more dramatically. Today I generate more than $25,000 in income a year from hobby."

Carole's hobbies were restoring her 1873 Victorian home, gourmet cooking, and being active in her local historical society. Carole would have Victorian summer tea parties and invite friends to come in costumes and live for a day as they did around the turn of the century. Guests played croquet and ate tea sandwiches, scones, and desserts made from period recipes. She invested a great deal of time and income restoring her home, buying books, traveling around the United States, England, and France doing research on tea products and presentations, taking photographs, and buying costumes, antique dishes, and linens. She began to generate income from her hobby by giving presentations on tea at local libraries, historical societies, and museums. She then began giving cooking lessons in the restored kitchen of her home. After class, the students would have tea in her garden, on the porch, or in front of the fire in the parlor, depending on the season. Women loved it! She started a newsletter to market the cooking classes and provide a calendar of her speaking engagements. Soon a book followed entitled *How to Serve a Proper Victorian Tea*. More books and videos are in progress. A fine gourmet restaurant in her hometown hired her to consult with them on a series of monthly theme teas. They used Carole's name, reputation, and newsletter to market those teas.

When you seem to be running low on possibilities of ways to turn your hobby to profit, consider hiring a consultant to spend an hour with you. I have found the return on that investment to be quite beneficial.

Possibilities with GRACE

So, now you have many possibilities to consider for producing income from your hobby. As you do, review them with GRACE:

God: He is first in all things: Add God to that "RACE" and you achieve GRACE.

You say you have a calling in this business?
Who is the Caller?
—Ken Blanchard, author of
The One-Minute Manager

Resilience: Get up when you're down. You conquer by continuing.

When you see a storm is coming,
see the lightning part the sky,
There's no place to run,
there's terror in your eye.
What you do then is to tell yourself
to wait it out and say,
"It's the storm, not me
that's bound to go away!"
—"Hold On," from the musical
The Secret Garden, lyrics by Marsha Norman

Action: It is not enough to dream; wake up and work at it!

Problems are only opportunities in workclothes.

—Henry John Kaiser (1882–1967),
American industrialist who oversaw
the construction of major highways,
bridges, and dams, including the
Grand Coulee Dam (1942). His
shipyards produced more than 1,400
vessels during World War II.

Creativity: Allow the unusual to happen. God gave us this gift and it is OK to use it.

Creativity is not determined by the kind of work . . .
but by the kind of approach taken to any job. It is
people, not jobs, who are creative.

—Robert M. Fulmer,
The New Management

Enthusiasm: Allow the spirit of excitement to fill you and spread to your friends. It is contagious and delightfully enriching.

So we must learn how to utilize enthusiasm in order to
move into that exciting and creative segment of the
human race—the achievers. You will find among them
total agreement that enthusiasm is the priceless
ingredient of personality that helps to achieve
happiness and self-fulfillment.

—Norman Vincent Peale,
Enthusiasm Makes the Difference

PART 2

THE PLAN

Going from Free to Fee

A businessman, a Baptist preacher, and a Boy Scout needed to get to Chicago from Huntsville. All the airlines were sold out. A private pilot offered to fly them for a very high price. They agreed.

Nearly to Chicago the pilot came on the speaker, "Unfortunately we have a problem and we are going to have to parachute out of the plane. Even more unfortunately, we only have three parachutes. Since I am taking one of them, the three of you can decide who gets the other two."

The businessman said, "Since I'm the smartest man in the world, I'm taking one." He put it on and jumped out the door.

The Baptist preacher, smiling bravely, said to the Boy Scout, "Son, you go ahead and take the other one. I know that I'm going to heaven when I die. Besides that, I've lived a long full life; I want you to take that parachute and jump."

The boy scout replied, "Oh, Preacher, don't worry about it, we'll be fine. The smartest man in the world just jumped out of the airplane with my backpack slipped around his shoulders."

No matter how smart you are, jumping into your dreams without first becoming a master planner can be a jump into disaster! If you start your business with a random plan, you can expect random results.

CHAPTER FIVE

Plan the Work and Work the Plan

Dreams and visions become reality when you plan the work and work the plan. You will find your mind racing with passion in the wee hours of the night, thinking of new and creative plans for additional strategies. Don't forget to do it with GRACE.

Most people don't plan to fail; but they fail to plan. Planning with GRACE has always been my secret. First I ask God to help me see his will in my decisions. Pray all the time for strength and for doors to open. Ask God to guide your dreams and to give you the fortitude and perseverance to plan carefully every step and every day.

With his strength, you will be able to be resilient. Your first plans might not materialize; however, don't quit. Don't ever quit planning for your dreams to become true. "If at first you don't succeed, join the club." Most of us didn't succeed with our first business dreams.

I act. Activity without the insight of a well-thought-out plan provides disaster. But a well-thought-out plan without activity is worse; it is nothing. Planning and action (work!) are probably more important than the dream. Daily you must take action to make your dreams become reality. As Will Rogers told us, "Plans get you into things but you got to work your way out."

I have always tried to think of creative ways to make the plans come true. When God closes a door to me, there is a great reason. I look for the window. I often feel a bit smug when I think of something creative and see that window opening. Then I remember with gratitude whose hand has opened it for me.

In all levels of designing and executing my plans, I am enthusiastic! The enthusiasm drives my plans forward and gives me the energy to create better plans.

> *May he give you the desire of your heart*
> *and make all your plans succeed.*
> —Psalm 20:4

Go from Free to Fee

You have spent your time, money, and energy on your hobby. Now you are ready to make a plan to get from free to fee. Before you are able to charge someone else a fee for anything, you must first believe you're truly worth a fee. I think Jessie Rittenhouse (1869–1948) put it best:

> I bargained with Life for a penny,
> And Life would pay no more.
> However I begged at evening
> When I counted my scanty store;
> For Life is a just employer,
> He gives you what you ask,
> But once you have set your wages,
> Why you must bear the task.
> I worked for a menial's hire,
> Only to learn dismayed,
> That any wage I had asked of Life
> Life would have gladly paid!

I freely gave advice on designing and sewing garments in my store while I was selling customers fabrics and laces. To help sell more products and merchandise, I began giving classes. This is where my paid sewing consulting began. I charged appropriately for my advice and was able to vastly increase sales in the store.

Putting a value on your time and your knowledge does not mean that you never give anything away. Soon others were looking at my success and asking me to help them. For many years I gave my "How to Run a Successful Business" seminars free to the sewing industry; many new accounts opened up to me because of these seminars.

Selling my advice now falls into two categories: (1) sewing advice and techniques, and (2) business advice and selling techniques. I have spent a lifetime developing these sewing and business seminars and I am able to charge for them. "Free seminars" were a monumental building block to bring about this "for a fee" time in my career.

Another way I was able to go from free to fee was to sell advice through my books. I have never resented the price of a book that brought me pleasure and new skills; apparently my customers feel the same way since we have sold more than 350,000!

It will be hard for you to go to those currently in your circle and get them to pay for your services. You have proven to them over the years that your service was one that was not worthy of a wage. I suggest you create a new market for yourself as you strive to go from free-to-fee work.

As you develop this new market, you will need to firmly keep in mind Jessie Rittenhouse's advice: For any wage you asked of life, life will gladly pay! You just need to ask.

How to Develop a Business Plan

You don't create a business without creating a pattern. To do that you must create the vision and work on it, or as my grandmother used to say, plan the work and work the plan.

Creating Your Vision: Written Goals

Some men see things as they are and say why.
I dream things that never were and say, why not?
—Robert F. Kennedy,
former U.S. senator

Before you worry about how to get there, you need to have some idea of where you want to go. This starts with a dream. Every dream precedes the goal.

Creativity, dreams (without a plan), and one dollar will buy you a cup of coffee in some places. Plans in one's head aren't worth much. *Write them down.* No business should begin without a written plan. Don't worry, most people don't know how to write a business plan. Just get a pen and paper, a computer, or a typewriter and write any thought you have about your business. Write at least three pages of plans, thoughts, and ideas a day for a month. Don't worry about what form the writing takes; just focus on writing at least three pages per day for thirty days of your plans, ideas, dreams, hopes, and possibilities.

A business dream must have the sort of natural enthusiasm that is all-consuming in your mind. Your ideas and hopes should pour out of you. If they don't, it means you aren't excited and interested enough in starting a business. If you're not able to write at least three pages a day for thirty days you probably don't need to go into business at all; your dreams are just a passing fantasy. A passing fantasy is temporary; a business is a lifestyle.

From these ninety pages of ideas and thoughts you will be able to build a simple outline. Don't worry about getting a fancy business plan like the big companies have. Former president of France, Charles de Gaulle, said, "It is better to have a bad plan than to have no plan at all." The business plan is a flexible document that will change and get better as your business grows. The more years you spend on it, the better, smarter, and more realistic it will get.

The following are questions you should answer as part of your ninety (or more!) pages of ideas and notes:

- How much money do you want to make the first year?
- What is your objective? What is it that you really want to do?
- Give a detailed description of the business.

- Explain the type of business.
- List all possible profit centers.
- Discuss the product/service offered.
- Discuss the advantages over your competitors.
- How is this venture unique?
- List the skills and experience you bring to the business.
- How will you acquire any additional needed skills and experience?
- What name will you go by?
- Discuss the ownership of the business and the legal structure.
- Where will the business be located? Why?
- What kind of facilities will you need?
- What kind of supplies?
- What kind of equipment?
- To produce your product or service, what steps are required?
- Where will you get supplies?
- Will you need employees? How many? What will your employees do?
- What are your plans for employee salaries, wages, and benefits?
- Discuss how you will hire your employees and discuss personnel procedures.
- Discuss lease or rent agreements.
- What insurance coverage will be needed?
- What licenses and permits will you need?
- What are your potential funding sources? How will you spend it?
- What financing will you need?
- How will the loans be secured?
- How much money do you want to make in the first year?
- What are the tax advantages of owning your own business?
- What are the requirements for making this business a legitimate business for the IRS?

- What is your total estimated business income for the first year?
- What are your total estimated business expenses, by month, for the first year?
- What will the return on the investment be?
- Why do you think this is a good risk?
- Discuss deadlines for each stage of your business. Set timetables. Be realistic.
- Explain pricing strategy for your product or service.
- Discuss your break-even point.
- Discuss how and who will maintain your accounting records.
- Evaluate your personal monthly financial needs.
- Explain your personal balance sheet and method of compensation.
- Explain how the business will be managed on a day-to-day basis.
- Who are the experts you might contact for advice?
- What are the alternatives when things go wrong? Provide "what if" statements to demonstrate alternative approaches to addressing any negatives that may develop.
- Who will your main customers be, the people you will sell to?
- Where might you buy possible mailing lists to reach these potential customers?
- Explain how your product/service will be advertised.
- Discuss how your product/service will be delivered.
- Discuss your potential customers.
- Discuss your competitors.
- Discuss how your competitors bring in customers.
- Do you feel that God is leading you to start a business?

As your pages of notes and ideas grow, you will begin to see plans and directions emerge. For instance, you will see you need to talk to the nice folks at city hall, the courthouse, the county government, etc. Include the results of these meetings.

Your notes on business licenses and procedures will greatly expand and enhance your plans and directions.

Working the Vision into a Business Plan

Life is too short to be little. Man is never so manly as when he feels deeply, acts boldly, and expresses himself with frankness and with fervour.
—Benjamin Disraeli (1804–81),
English statesman, author

I was able to get a small one-thousand-square-foot space at the end of a shopping center. The rent was $500 per month in 1981. As I stood there looking at a bare room, I was appalled to realize I had already spent all of our savings on the inventory. We dragged all of the fixtures we could spare from our house and bought a few more at antique stores and garage sales. Obviously my original budget for inventory should have included much more than inventory for a retail store. Little did I know how much it would cost to get shelving, wallpaper, carpet, fixtures, a cash register, and a checkout area. Joe paid for all of this—another angel when I needed one. I suggest you do better than I did at creating that first business plan!

A business plan includes the answers to all of the questions asked in the previous section. Take those ninety pages of notes and make a plan! Your local Small Business Administration has forms and guides for business plan outlines. These are also available on the Internet. Don't forget the library and bookstores.

A good solid written plan will benefit you in these ways:

- Writing it out often unearths advantages, new opportunities, and deficiencies in your plan. It will assist in identifying your customers, your market area, your pricing strategy, and how to be competitive in each.
- It will help you identify the amount of funds you will need, and when you will need them.

- Lenders and investors will assess your business savvy by your business plan. A solid plan will be the basis for a financing proposal and show you off as a business manager and a good risk.
- Putting plans to paper will help you look ahead and avoid problems before they arise.
- The plan acts as a reality check.

A river without banks is a large puddle.
Power comes with direction.
—Ken Blanchard,
American businessman and
business/management author

How to Work the Plan

Some people dream, others stay awake and live those dreams! Work on your plan and your plan will work for you. In this section I will give you tips to focus, to organize your dreams and your time, and to overcome procrastination when you start to fall away from working on your plan.

Focus

I have always thought that one man of tolerable
abilities may work great changes, and accomplish
great affairs among mankind, if he first forms a good
plan, and, cutting off all amusements or other
employments that would divert his attention, make the
execution of that same plan his sole study and business.
—Benjamin Franklin (1706–90),
U.S. statesman, writer

The first step in working your plan is to work on your focus. Focus with GRACE, God first in all things, Resilience,

Action, Creativity, and Enthusiasm. Keep your mind on where you want to go, for "as [a man] thinketh in his heart, so is he" Prov. 23:7a, KJV."

Wayne Gretsky is considered perhaps the greatest hockey star in the history of the sport. He is the only professional player to score more than fifty goals in fifty-or-less games in a single year. And he has done it year after year, as well as leading the league in scoring. When asked his secret, Gretsky replies, "I skate to where the puck is going to be, not where it has been."

When you focus with grace on your dream, not only will you walk toward it with a faster and stronger stride, but those around you will be more eager to support you.

If the trumpet does not sound a clear call,
who will get ready for battle?
—1 Corinthians 14:8

Refocus

What business are you really in? I hear you saying, "Martha, why didn't I need to ask myself that before I got started?" But you don't really know what is going to work and pay well and what you will enjoy doing until you get into it. As you work and rework your plan, ask yourself, "What business am I really in?" Profits will improve dramatically when you do. As Tom Peters pointed out, railroad companies almost went out of business because they didn't stop to ask themselves this vital question. If they had only realized they were in the transportation business, instead of the train business, they would have gone into air transport as it grew.

Micki Voisard's hobby was hiking and spending time in nature. Sometimes her grandfather would come along and they would be gone for hours "just looking around." When she was only twelve years old, Micki began making "fort furniture," inspired by the wilderness she loved, out of the manzanita wood surrounding their ranch. It was crude stuff, but everyone in her family got a piece of it for birthdays and Christmas. "I always wondered how many Salvation Army stores have received my unwanted pieces!"

Over the years, she perfected her carving skills and always carved an animal on the furniture piece. She did craft shows, indoor and outdoor, for many years. Micki realized there was a huge difference in price between the craft and the fine art market, so she asked herself, "What business am I really in?" She began to position her work as a finely handcrafted product that needed to get into a more sophisticated market. "Once I read in a wood-working magazine that Daniel Mack, the father of the return of rustic furniture, was looking for 'stickers' (one who works with wood, creating furniture in an untraditional way) to put in his new book. So I contacted him. I made it into his first book! Getting in a book doesn't guarantee anything, but it gives you credibility and makes you an 'expert.' Before long my status changed—now I do major fine art shows."

Soon Micki made a major shift to whimsical carved animal sculptures. Her sales went up dramatically. She then incorporated public speaking with her art to help promote sales. She also began having her most popular woodcarvings bronzed. This gives her limited editions of her work, which increases her income and also opens up another market for her. "I feel I have been successful because I have good visionary skills. I used to think it was because I was good at marketing. That is true, but marketing doesn't help you if you're marketing heavily in Japan and they're going through a bad recession. It doesn't mean you ignore Japan, but you reroute your ideas to some other area where the financial climate is better. This is a constant; one has to adjust to that thinking. I believe it's important to keep growing. If you're primarily doing the same art you were ten years ago without branching out in some way then you have become stale and are not keeping up with the times we live in. There is a lot of dispute on that, but for me personally it works to periodically make a paradigm shift. Today I generate $65,000 to

$75,000 a year and will probably increase that with the new avenue of bronzing my work."

When you stop to ask yourself what business you are really in, you will often find you change your plan in wonderful new and profitable directions.

A Stitch in Time Saves Nine! Organize Your Dreams

From your business plan you will discover the thousands of tiny steps needed to accomplish your plan. These will be your short- and long-term plans. I find writing them down helps tremendously with my focus. I heard Robert Schuller say, "Yard by yard, life is hard: but inch by inch, it's a cinch." Writing down each step you will need to take, and when you intend to take it, is an inch-by-inch process that makes turning your dream into reality a cinch!

In my seminars I love to use an audience participation exercise to illustrate the need to organize your dreams, inch by inch. I ask everyone to blow up a balloon and hold it above his/her head. When I count to three I ask everyone to release the balloon. Hundreds of balloons whip around the crowd, dashing everywhere with great enthusiasm, but no plan! Then I ask everyone to blow up a second balloon. This time we take an extra step before just letting loose our dreams: we tie a knot in the bottom. Now the balloons go where we want them to go. They can be passed from individual to individual with relative ease. They can even be caught and held quietly. Your plan for your business, your plan for life, your plan for the day's accomplishment will flow with a complete list before the work day begins.

Making a list is one of the most, if not *the* most, critical factor in my business life today. Without that daily list, I am lost and nothing gets done. Confusion and frustration sets in. I feel my fuse becoming shorter and I don't like that feeling, nor do my colleagues. I like tied-balloon days better than those crazy-balloon days. It is a magic technique that can make the difference between your success and failure.

Being organized not only makes you get where you want to go, it makes you more likeable to other executives and business owners. My friend Ann Taylor, a very successful artist and a former executive with a major cosmetic company, gave me advice on how to make a successful phone call. She always organizes her phone calls and begins like this: "Hello, Martha, this is Ann Taylor, how are you?" I reply the usual. She then says, "I know you are busy and I only have three things to talk with you about. First, _____." She briefly discusses each item, then thanks me for my time and gets off the phone. Period. I think Ann can probably get into anyone's office for a call because everyone knows that her calls are organized.

Project Sheets

Your mind is like a computer; it needs very specific instructions and directions, not just vague and random ideas. Writing your plans out on a project or dream sheet helps you define them, learn about them, and seriously consider them as believable or achievable.

Now, you take the items and ideas in your project sheet and schedule them into your life.

Schedule Your Time

Each person has to define short- and long-term plans. Forget the business book definitions; you are the author of your own business book. I keep my plans in my "organizer," but I have been known to keep them on a legal pad or in a spiral binder. However you keep yours, don't lose it, and keep it with you!

Here is how I plan my hours, weeks, months, and years:

1. today's "to-do list"
2. short-term plans
3. long-term plans
4. really long-term plans
5. delegated tasks

PROJECT SHEET

PROJECT _____

- Amount of sales I want from this particular profit center or project
  $_____

- People involved in this project

- Brainstorming for achieving this dollar amount project. In other words, how will I reach my financial goal?

- How to market this project

- More possible tasks for completing this project

Today's "To-Do List"

- phone calls to return
- people to have private meetings with
- what to schedule; what to turn down
- answering immediate crises
- delegating what I can

Short-Term Plans

Monthly plans as well as three-month plans fall in this category.

- deadlines on books
- deadlines on materials and samples arriving in Huntsville
- advertising deadlines
- plans for television series
- written sections in books
- art work for books
- materials sent ahead for seminars
- having private meetings with individuals to check on how their projects are coming
- private meetings with finance staff to see where we are
- private meetings with shipping staff to check on numbers, up or down
- private meetings for new ideas on expansion or improvement
- projects I need to be writing
- editing I need to be doing
- new books—gathering data and writing

Long-Term Plans

Long-range plans help you get past short-term obstacles. In my planning, a long-term plan means longer than three months and up to five years.

- plan new expansion by looking at possible markets
- plan new written products
- plan where seminars will be

- plan how many large seminars to have in Huntsville
- plan catalog entries and dates to mail catalog
- plan new curriculum for schools in the future
- plan new markets to send television shows
- plan new public relations campaigns as well as advertising
- evaluate where we are on all current projects
- with finance people, plan where we would like to be in sales by the end of the year. Discuss where we could expand to meet that plan.

Really Long-Term Plans

Plans mean nothing if they don't excite you. For me this means completely new avenues of business. Some of the really long-term plans I set for myself, that are now part of my everyday reality, are/were:

- the television series
- expanding the retail mail order business
- writing a business book
- speaking and training seminars on small business
- seminars overseas
- expanding into the doll industry
- larger women's dress patterns

Delegated Tasks

Delegate everything you can to other people, and ask them to follow up with you. Then make a list to be sure that the tasks were completed and followed up with you. Soon you will learn who can be trusted 100 percent to do what you asked and who forgets!

Carry a Written Planning System

Start organizing yourself and your business with an "organizer." If you don't have one, get one now! Begin to use it faithfully and you will understand what I am saying. I have heard that charts are effective for some people, but I need my organizer with me so I can add and enhance items as I think of them. I open my "book" while I'm driving, sitting in airports, in the drive-through at fast-food restaurants. Sometimes a great idea grabs me in the middle of the night and I reach over to my trusty list and write it down!

Customers are impressed when you have all of your information with you and can make commitments on the spot. Write down ideas that others have shared with you. It is a great way to bond with customers and team members (not to mention it acts as a reminder to do what you say you will do!). I also write down phone, fax, and E-mail numbers as soon as I hear them.

Next comes the question, "Do you *always* have your book with you?" The answer is no. But I always carry my purse and I keep a small spiral notebook in it. I write down ideas in that small book when I don't have my big organizer. This way it is always with me for quick reference. Too many plans are written down at a seminar on a notepad and then carefully filed away—permanently—never to be seen again! When I get back to my planner, I take my little spiral notebook and transfer the information.

My planner contains:

- three-year calendar
- address book
- project sheets
- telephone numbers
- month-by-month planning
- monthly calendar
- daily planning sheets

My Organizer Magic Tricks

Here are my suggestions for getting the most out of your organizer:

- Schedule everything that needs a schedule. You need to set a completion date for all your plans and write them in your organizer.
- Write tentative date or plans in pencil.
- Keep your commitments!

- Take it with you everywhere.
- Plan several years in advance. Use your planning system every day, all day long.
- Get the year-at-a-glance box pull-out sheet for current year and future years. Always carry a two-year calendar with you and write down all tentative and definite commitments.
- Use the month-at-a-glance boxes for at least two years in advance.
- Use the daily plan sheets for your daily to-do list.
- Put what didn't get done today on tomorrow's to-do list.
- Use color-coded, tabbed sections behind the monthly calendars for your project sheets. For example, I have one for books in progress, volunteer work, and future expansion.
- Have a brainstorming section in the back with completely wild ideas that may have no merit whatsoever. You never know.
- During the holiday season I have a gift list.
- Mark off each task as it is completed.
- Write a phone number and the person's name beside all messages and commitments.
- Note all of the items you will need during the day to accomplish the tasks on your to-do list. This will help prioritize your tasks.
- Work by importance rather than urgency.

My Favorite Time-Savers

I would I could stand on a busy corner, hat in hand,
and beg people to throw me all their wasted hours.
—Bernard Berenson

Here are a few of my favorite timesaving tips:

- Use a written planning system and have it with you at all times. Never be without it.
- Spend the first thirty minutes of every day with a pencil, pen, or computer and your planner.

- Write and type: Have the daily planner and the computer open at all times and write or type like crazy whenever a thought occurs to you. Don't let a good idea get away.

- Write it down: Writing relieves anxiety; for me it is almost as good as accomplishing the task. Without a written plan, I feel as if loose ends aren't tied up at the end of each day.

- Unclutter your work surfaces on a regular basis, probably daily. Don't handle something more than once. Deal with it by forcing yourself to do one of three options: Do, Dump, or Delegate!

- Use a file cabinet for everything; if you don't know what you are going to do with a document, put it on your list and file it where you can put your hands on it later.

- Before going home for the day, completely clear your desk of the clutter.

- Give yourself fifteen minutes of wrap-up time at the end of each day. While problems and solutions are fresh in your mind, write down notes on your to-do lists.

- Those things you can't Do, Dump, or Delegate, put on one of your "lists." Procrastination is a killer. Make that list and follow it.

- Delegate everything you can to someone else, and then make a list to be sure that it was done.

- Set deadlines for all tasks and call a private meeting to see how employees are coming along on meeting those deadlines.

- Before you call, write down what you want to cover. Don't waste time trying to think of everything you want to say.

- Return calls late in the afternoon.

- Avoid phone tag. The message on your telephone answering system must ask for a complete message. Also, it should update your callers on your location and schedule.

- Reduce "go between" phone calls with conference calls. They will also reduce the total time spent in communication and in misunderstandings. When using conference calls, make sure everyone involved knows in advance so they will be prepared.

- Have individual staff meetings rather than large ones. A ten-minute private meeting accomplishes much more than a forty-five-minute public meeting with the whole staff.
- Don't forget to move old files to a storage place on a regular basis. Add new space as needed.
- E-mail is the way to communicate in a fast, economical manner. It is time for you to get on-line! If Martha Pullen, who never thought she would use a laptop, can log on and conduct business through her E-mail, then anyone can! E-mail is inexpensive, more reliable, and much faster than regular mail.
- Plan your personal life also, since you won't have much of it if it isn't organized.
- Get up at 5 A.M. rather than 6 A.M.!

Those who make the worst use of their time
are the first to complain of its brevity.
—La Bruyère (1645–1696),
French writer, moralist, and satirist

Use Wait Times Effectively

Make the most of every minute—especially while you are waiting. You can utilize wait times to help accomplish your tasks for the day.

- Car wait time: Car phones are a great way to use commute time to your advantage.
- Airport wait time: I put business papers in a pull-on case, which makes a dandy laptop desk while I wait to board the plane.
- Flying wait times: I do much of my planning and project development on an airplane. Take a laptop computer and get it out again as soon as you are allowed to. (Always

have an extra battery for your laptop because sometimes you can't find an outlet to recharge.)

- In-line wait time: If you suspect you are going to be stuck in a line, bring along something to read, like those magazines and trade journals you keep putting off.
- Phone wait times: Keep several pads of paper on your desk to jot down ideas while on hold.

Plan Productive Time

Without an organized planning time each week, each day, my work probably won't get too far. I have read that Mary Kay Ash requires her directors to spend at least four hours per week behind closed doors with absolutely no disturbance. As your life gets busier, these times will become harder to create. You can train those around to leave you alone during a certain time of day. But it will be most effective if that time is when you are least needed. Try for early in the morning or late at night. Give yourself an hour of strict work time, close your door, and let your voice mail get your incoming calls.

Discourage Interruptions

- Close the door: My staff knows that I want no one to disturb me other than my mother, husband, or one of my children.
- Screened calls: My staff screens my calls carefully. They explain that I am in an "important closed door meeting," but they ask for a full message of what the caller would like from me. If my staff thinks I need to know, they interrupt me.
- Knock: People are more reluctant to disturb me if they know they need to knock first.

Overcoming Procrastination

Procrastination is opportunity's natural assassin.
—Victor Kiam, CEO and President of Remington Products

"I'm not very enthusiastic about this task. I'll just do this later."

Sound familiar? Many of us never plan the dream and work the plan because we wait for . . . what? Let's just call it what it is, *procrastination*. Once we get up the gumption to begin, we procrastinate about many of the little steps along the way. Soon we are merely keeping up with yesterday, thanks to procrastination.

Which comes first, motivation or productive action? Do you wait until you feel like doing something? Or do you take action whether you feel like it or not? Procrastinators wait for the mood to strike them before tackling a task. I am afraid there is no other solution to being a success in business than to just dive right into productive action, whether the mood is there or not. Get started regardless of your feelings and your fears.

My Model for Procrastination Eradication!

Putting off an easy thing makes it hard,
and putting off a hard one makes it impossible.
—George H. Lorimer , former
editor-in-chief, *Saturday Evening Post*

I wish I had a dime for every time I have said, "I should get to that," or "I ought to do this right now but I really don't feel like it," or "Oh, I can do that anytime."

I procrastinate because I fear something. Years ago Dr. Marion Gallaway at the University of Alabama told me, "If you ever prepare to stand in front of an audience and you don't have butterflies, then don't go on; you don't really care about your performance." I have remembered this for the last thirty years. As the time approaches for me to meet a new audience, I begin to think of excuses to procrastinate and avoid giving the talk. Why? Fear. Yes, fear. After more than one thousand presentations, I still get nervous. The morning when I am going to meet my audience, I procrastinate as long as possible and walk in at the last minute.

Shortly after the morning begins, I begin to feel better. Once I overcome the fear that is causing me to procrastinate, some very nice things begin to happen. Someone usually tells me she has been saving her money for many months just so she can be with me today. Another will tell me that watching the television show is the happiest part of her week. A third one will say that she is caring for a sick husband, but that looking forward to this seminar has made the last few months bearable. Another might tell me that she couldn't afford to come; however, her friend bought her ticket as a special surprise. As they get excited my enthusiasm builds, and I know I am doing what I am supposed to be doing. Far from that dragging procrastinator of the morning, I run excitedly around the room looking at their projects. We all become so filled with joy, we hug and laugh over their accomplishments. At the end of the day I am exhausted, but I am looking forward to the second day!

My fears caused major procrastination in writing this book. I knew that I had a lot to say to those with a dream of opening a business from their hobby. I just couldn't begin. Day after day I procrastinated. I would tell myself, "Oh, Martha, you don't know how to write this type of book. Wait until you have learned more about business. Maybe take a course in business at the university."

Finally, I had the good sense to purchase a book on how to write a book. I read the silliest section which said, "To write a book, just begin to write. Write three pages a day no matter if you have an interesting thought or not. Don't try to organize or plan anything. Just write three pages per day for one month. It doesn't matter what you write, just write."

I began to write three pages a day. I took my computer with me and wrote on the airplane and in hotel rooms. I wrote on Sunday after church. At the end of the month I had ninety pages.

Funny, I began to like what I was doing. Even when I wasn't "in the mood to write," writing actually put me in the mood!

I wanted a cowriter who had been through this experience before and knew how to take all my ideas and put them into a book. I called Lilly Walters. I loved her style on her previous books, she loved me, and our relationship was sealed!

This book wouldn't be in your hands right now if I had waited until I could have written a perfect book on business. There is no such thing!

What may be done at any time will be done at no time.
—Scottish proverb

Tips to Conquer Procrastination

- I always put my "should" and "ought to's" on a list; writing them down makes them almost commands.
- I write down a job I have been procrastinating. I make two lists: one of the reasons to put this job off further and one of the reasons to go ahead and do this job. This normally puts me in the right frame of mind to take action and either Do, Dump, or Delegate.
- Write down absolutely all the steps needed to get this task done.
- Order this list from most important to least important. Tackle the highest priority items first.
- Delegate all items on the list, if possible. Make a list or note telling to whom the task was delegated. Track in your organizer when you need to follow up with that person. Even the best teams and suppliers need to know you are on top of things.
- If you don't do the step today, put it at the top of tomorrow's list. Don't scratch it off until you either Do, Dump, or Delegate it.
- It's OK to "Just Say No." Rather than feeling like I am lazy or an unworthy person because I don't do certain activities, I need to recognize that I can't be good at

everything. Besides, it isn't my responsibility to do everything well. As much as I like my house very clean, I don't like to clean my house! Rather than condemning myself for that, I should admit it and either pay someone else to clean my house or do it myself with full recognition that I hate cleaning house.

> *If I were to suggest a general rule for*
> *happiness, I would say "Work a little*
> *harder; work a little longer; Work!"*
> —Frederick H. Ecker

Procrastination Is Handled Best with GRACE

First give it to **G**od. He'll give you ideas and the ambition to get it done.

Be **R**esilient. You will meet roadblocks to getting the task done, go around them, go over them, go under them—but go!

Take **A**ction! As Arthur Godfrey said, "Even if you're on the right track—you'll get run over if you just sit there."

Be **C**reative in dealing with procrastination. Find some aspect of the task that catches your interest.

Act **E**nthusiastic, and you become enthusiastic.

CHAPTER SIX

The Business of the Hobby Business

One of the ways you can profit from turning your hobby into a business is using it as a write-off. Beware! Talk to your accountant. The IRS is especially on the lookout for those "fudging" to make a hobby appear as a business. You must be actually working on turning your hobby to profit for the IRS to accept your losses as deductions. This means business permits and licenses, accounting, and records. Even then, you must make a profit three out of every five years. This will change from state to state and year to year—ask your accountant.

In this section I will cover where to find information vital to running your business, financing, permits and licensing, insurance, taxes, accounting, records, contracts, agreements, and collections.

Where to Find Information Vital to Running Your Business

If a blind man leads a blind man,
both will fall into a pit.
—Matthew 15:14b

Information is power! Without it, you will be like the blind trying to lead the blind. Make it your business to know what business information is available, where to get it, and most importantly, how to use it. You will need to know more than just your specific area of business. You will need to know about business licenses, employee hiring and firing laws, etc.

You probably have many of the skills necessary to run a business from your other life experiences—raising a family, teaching, nursing, running an office for someone else, volunteering, or whatever other profession you have followed thus far. Take a good look at what you already know, then just make a good guess at what skills and knowledge you will need to turn your hobby into a profit center. Where do you find these?

- The library is the place to find books about how to run a business; how to get better at the specific skills you need to improve your craft; and what resources, associations, and publications are available to you in your field. Ask your reference librarian, a wonderful resource.
- Manufacturers and suppliers of small business technologies and products in your area are often willing to share ideas, resources, and offer advice.
- Others in your same line of work. Check the phone book.
- Trade associations of those in your type of craft or business hold education meetings, usually on local and national levels.
- State economic development agencies
- State department of commerce
- Your local county industrial development authority
- National Business Incubator Association (association made up of individuals who run facilities that assist start-up companies. They provide shared secretarial services, low-cost rental space, fax service, Internet connections, professional advisors, etc.)
- Chambers of commerce
- Local colleges
- U.S. Small Business Administration is a must for the information you will need to run your business. Through workshops, individual counseling, publications, and videotapes, the SBA helps entrepreneurs understand and meet the challenges of starting a business, including financing, marketing, and management. Other help the SBA provides include the following:
  - SCORE: More than 12,400 volunteers in the Service Corps of Retired Executives provide training and

one-on-one counseling at no charge. I had a volunteer retired businessman who came to me and helped me in many aspects of my business. He didn't charge one cent and his advice and encouragement were wonderful!

- Small business development centers provide training, counseling, research, and other specialized assistance at nearly one thousand locations nationwide.

- SBA's business information centers (BICs) provide state-of-the-art computers, graphic workstations, CD-ROM technology, and interactive videos for accessing market research databases, planning and spreadsheet software, and a vast library of information. With the BIC library and software, you can craft your own business and marketing plans.

- SBA's One Stop Capital Shops gather federal, state, and local agencies and institutions in one convenient location to address the financial and technical assistance needs of small businesses.

- Small Business Institutes (SBIs)

Check your telephone directory under U.S. Government for your local SBA office or call the Small Business Answer Desk at 1-800-8-ASK-SBA for information. Also, you may request a free copy of *The Small Business Directory*, a listing of business development publications and videotapes, from your local SBA office or the Answer Desk.

To find the local SBA Web sites, use a search engine on the Internet. The SBA national Web Site is located at http://www.sbaonline.sba.gov/.

Financing Your Dreams

Many businesses that had ample financial backing failed. Many excelled with almost no funds at all. There is something about knowing you must succeed that forces you to succeed! Yet knowing how much things will really cost to run and working on ways to bring in sufficient start-up capital can smooth the path on your journey.

Things always cost more than we think they will. Estimate very high in your projected costs. Go back to the earlier section "How to Develop a Business Plan" on pages 53–57 and note the list of questions there. These will help you think through what items you need to include in your estimated costs. Hire an accountant, if you can afford one in the first stages of your business, to help you estimate your cash flow needs.

Where to Find the Money

Once you know how much money you will need, you must find ways to bring in enough to operate your business while you are making it profitable.

- committing your own funds (This is a great indicator to others of how serious you are about your business.)
- family members or a partner
- banks
- commercial finance companies
- venture capital firms
- local development companies
- life insurance companies
- trade credit
- selling stock
- Small Business Administration (SBA)

SBA Assistance in Financing

The Small Business Administration is a great place to start when you need a loan. They have new programs all the time. You will find useful information about the small business loans from a local office, and even more easily at their web site (http//www.sbaonline.sba.gov/business_finances/). The following is a sample of the information available on the day we checked in: (When you visit the site it will surely be different. Make decisions about your business based on current information.)

- SBA's size standards
- Additional financial resources and information
- Office of Advocacy ACE-Net—investor opportunities
- Small Business Investment Act of 1958 as amended September 96
- SBA now provides a Directory of Small Business Lending reported by commercial banks for 1994, 1995, and for 1996
- SBA now provides ready-to-complete loan application forms for downloading to your PC
- Procurement assistance and grants
- SBA financial assistance notices
- Shareware programs for financing a business
- Financing Your Business workshop

Financing Workshop Objectives

Credit Issues

SBA Loan Programs—
   Overview

Veterans

7(A) 11

Assistance for Physically
   Challenged

Contract Loan Program

Seasonal Line of Credit

Exporter's Revolving Line
   of Credit Program

Small General Contractors

Guaranteed Loans to
   Qualified Employee
   Trusts

Certified Development
   Companies (504)

International Trade Loan

Pollution Control Loan

Small Loan Program

Disaster Loan Program

Microloan Program

GreenLine Revolving Line of
   Credit

Summary of 7(a) Special
   Loans

Regular, Certified and
   Preferred Lenders

What Businesses Are
   Eligible?

How to Apply

APPENDIX: Application
   Forms

Entire Financing Workbook

Types of loans that might be available through the SBA:

- LowDoc: Designed to increase the availability of funds under $100,000 and streamline/expedite the loan review process.
- FA$TRAK: Designed to increase the capital available to businesses seeking loans up to $100,000 but is currently offered as a pilot with a limited number of lenders.
- CAPLines: An umbrella program to help small businesses meet their short-term and cyclical working-capital needs with five separate programs.
- International Trade: If your business is preparing to engage in or is already engaged in international trade, or is adversely affected by competition from imports, the International Trade Loan Program is designed for you.
- Export Working: Capital designed to provide short-term working capital to exporters in a combined effort of the SBA and the Export-Import Bank.
- Pollution Control: Designed to provide loan guarantees to eligible small businesses for the financing of the planning, design, or installation of a pollution-control facility.
- DELTA: Defense Loan and Technical Assistance is a joint SBA and Department of Defense effort to provide financial and technical assistance to defense-dependent small firms adversely affected by cutbacks in defense.
- Minority and Women's Prequal: A pilot program that uses intermediaries to assist prospective minority and women borrowers in developing viable loan application packages and securing loans.
- Disabled Assistance: The SBA has not been provided funding for direct handicapped assistance loans, but such individuals are eligible for all SBA loan guaranty programs.
- Qualified Employee Trusts: Designed to provide financial assistance to Employee Stock Ownership Plans.
- Veteran's Loans: The SBA has not been provided funds for direct loans to veterans, although veterans are eligible

for special considerations under SBA's guaranty loan programs.

- SBA's Microloan Program: This program works through intermediaries to provide small loans from as little as $100 up to $25,000.
- SBA's Certified Development Company (504 Loan) Program: This program, commonly referred to as the 504 program, makes long-term loans available for purchasing land, buildings, and machinery and equipment, and for building, modernizing, or renovating existing facilities and sites.
- SBA's Certified and Preferred Lenders Program
- SBA's Secondary Market Program
- SBA's Small Business Investment Company Program: Small Business Investment Companies (SBICs), which are licensed and regulated by the SBA, are privately owned and managed investment firms that provide venture capital and startup financing to small businesses.
- SBA's Surety Bond Program

Permits and Licensing

Where there is no vision, the people perish:
but he that keepeth the law, happy is he.
—Proverbs 29:18, KJV

Before you begin a factory in your backyard or a sewing shop in your garage, make sure you are operating with the right permits and licenses. You can be in for a rude shock when the nice people from the city knock at your door and try to close you down. Licenses, zoning laws, and other regulations vary from business to business and from state to state. For instance, if your hobby is skydiving and you are going to profit from it by teaching skydiving, you might set up an office in your garage from which to run the business and market it. You would then take people up in planes that take off from an airport. For this you would need to be a licensed trainer, possibly need a local business license, and a home occupancy permit. On the other hand, if you were going to publish a magazine or catalog about skydiving and you were going to mail it around the world or via the Internet, you probably wouldn't need a trainer's license or a local business license. We say "probably." It is important to check first, research all levels of government: city, county, state, and federal. Check with each branch and determine what you might need for:

- your specific type of business
- professional requirements
- doing business in general

Each location varies (some places have state and county requirements, some only state requirements, etc.). Things you must check to get started are:

- a business license
- a home occupancy permit (if working from home)
- a name registration
- a resale license from your home state

Generally, for typical small local businesses, call your local municipality, city, township, or county office. Each one will have information about other agencies you need to contact.

Try the white pages phone book and/or the information operator in your area, check listing under government, city hall, and especially anything that sounds like a business permit office. Telephone receptionists will direct your call to what they feel is appropriate within each government agency. Clerks will continue to pass you on until you reach the right place. Unfortunately, the clerks passing you along may or may not know what they are doing, so don't stop with just one person's advice. Asking others who do similar sorts of work in your area may give you some good ideas, but they may be operating illegally themselves and not realize it. Try checking with several, if not all, of the following about what sort of permits and licenses you need:

- your local Small Business Administration (SBA) office
- City Hall
- Chamber of Commerce
- state Department of Commerce
- local county Industrial Development Authority
- National Business Incubator Association
- your attorney for advice specific to your enterprise and area
- a Certified Public Accountant
- Economic Development Department[2]
- others who do similar sorts of work in your area
- business editors of the local media covering your area
- office of your elected representatives (Tell them you want to create jobs in their area—they'll help you!)

Insurance and Liability

You must talk with an attorney and a good insurance agent to find out just what your liability is in turning your hobby into a business. If your hobby is mushroom gathering, and you decide to teach others your craft, but someone picks the wrong mushroom and becomes ill, you will have a tremendous problem. You must seek expert help in how to protect yourself. When you pick an insurance agent, find one who specializes in business liability.

Taxes

The distinction between hobbies and a business becomes acute when dealing with losses. The law does not allow deduction of hobby-related losses, except to the extent that they offset hobby-related income. However, if you are running your hobby as a business, related losses are deductible. Unless you are happy with doing this type of research, I strongly suggest you hire an accountant to help render to Caesar what is his—and to keep you on the right side of the law!

Always check with your CPA about your specific situation before you try to deduct something from your taxes:

- Call the IRS: Call 1 (800) TAX-FORM. Ask for IRS publication 334. This booklet tells all the benefits that are available to you with a small, home-based business.

- Hire your spouse: By paying your spouse at least $2,000 a year, you will take money out of one pocket and put it into the other, creating a tax deduction that did not exist previously. You will also allow your spouse to establish an additional IRA. This is $2,000 more you can get into tax-deferred status.

- Hire your children: If you pay your children less than $4,000 a year (the standard exemption everybody enjoys), and they have no unearned income, they don't have to file a tax return. There is no FICA, FUTA, or workers compensation insurance and you don't lose them as dependents.

- Deduct your vehicles: The IRS allows you to deduct thirty-one cents a mile.

- Deduct your communication: your telephone, your cell phone, pager, and E-mail account.

- Invest in Section 179 assets: computers, fax machines, telephones, pagers, cell phones, desk, chairs, file cabinets, etc. IRC 179 allows you to deduct these assets, dollar per dollar, up to $18,000.

- Deduct books, periodicals, magazines, and newspapers: These are necessary items for the small business entrepreneur.

- Deduct business training: "Business" seminars are 100 percent tax deductible; "investment" seminars may not be.

- Make your vacation tax deductible by having your board meeting, seminar, or other trainings in a wonderful vacation spot. If you are fond of Tahoe, you might hold your meeting in Carson City, which is close by but not thought of as a vacation spot.

- List all your resources: Be clear on what you have to work with—cash, stocks, bonds, insurance, CDs, IRAs, your money partners, credit lines, and investment cards.[3] (For information on establishing your own self-directed IRA, visit Ray Como's website at http://www.raycomo.com.)

Accounting and Records

For me, keeping records is the least alluring of all aspects of running a business. But, alluring or not, you need records to run your business and increase profits—plus, it's the law! They are also mandatory for:

- federal and state tax returns, including income tax and Social Security laws
- getting credit and loans from vendors or banks
- substantiating the worth of your business, should you wish to sell it
- knowing what is profitable and what is not in your business

Your records will deal mainly with what your expenses are:

- supplies
- advertising
- location (rent, licenses)
- employee costs
- equipment

Bookkeeping Methods and Checking Accounts

Any stationery store can set you up with the proper paperwork. There are all kinds of simple software programs that make the process much easier, as well as classes on this at your local junior colleges and adult education centers. Hiring an accountant to walk you through your setup might be an excellent investment too.

Your first step to opening a business can be just opening a checking account. You will need a name for your business. Your banker can advise you on the laws and procedures in your area on opening a business checking account.

Easy Way to Do Expense Reports

Expense reports are vital, and a great hassle if you spend any time at all on the road. Let me tell you one of my secrets: Ziploc plastic bags! You have an expense report "bag" to keep all of those receipts for one trip. Label the bag with the date of the trip, the place, and the return date. You can also write *auto* or *plane*. If it is auto, write the beginning and ending mileage on these labels. If there are lots of receipts, you might use a large bag.

On another large label on the bag, you can write any expenses you wish to write. A separate bag for each trip is a good way not to lose receipts. When you get home you can put the receipts into proper forms.

What Kind of Business Entity Should You Be?

Basically, there are four types of business entities:

1. Sole Proprietorship
2. Partnership
3. Subchapter S Corporation
4. C Corporation

The Small Business Center (SBC) can provide handouts to explain these various types of business entities. A talk with an attorney or accountant will be in your future once you get your business moving.

Contracts, Agreements, and Collections

If you are taking orders of any type for a product or service, a contract between you and your customers is vital! A contract's main purpose is to help everyone remember what was agreed upon. Someone may contract for your services six months to two years ahead of the date. Many of us are in the business of taking an order, then delivering the goods on a specified date. I do this for my speaking engagements. We may book something a year in advance. Working that far out makes it easy to forget what everyone has agreed to, such as "free shipping of products." Many hobbyists forget they quoted a fee of $1,000 that covered labor plus materials. They submit the bill for $1,000 and add on a $750 materials charge, and the customer is outraged. No one is trying to be dishonest, but the human animal is just plain forgetful! Having all the terms spelled out and signed by both sides will also serve to remind you, many months down the line, of your side of the bargain.

On those occasions when your customer is not holding up his end of the bargain, and you decide to pursue satisfaction through the courts, you have a much better chance of getting a ruling in your favor if you have a written agreement. For instance, in dressmaking, an agreement would need to state at least the actual price to the customer for the dress, the style of the dress with any special additions you have discussed, grade and type materials you will use, the terms of payment, the date the garment will be delivered, how it will be delivered and who pays for delivery costs, the number of fittings necessary, and the terms if a fitting is canceled.

A nonrefundable deposit of 25 to 75 percent is expected for almost any product or service, with the balance made payable on the date of the delivery. Having a deposit up front is a great way to weed out customers who are not serious.

Agreements do not always need to be formal, legal-looking documents. A letter, stating the terms, with a place for your customer and you to sign, will do. This, by the way, is legally binding. An agreement may be as simple as an "order form," including the terms of payment and a description of what you will give to your customer.

Begin reading the contracts you are asked to sign almost daily. There are terms specified in all kinds of things. Note every time you sign a credit card slip! Note what sorts of terms others are asking for in the business world.

You can get sample contracts, order forms, invoices, and/or letters of agreement from:

- any stationery or office supply store
- software programs, even most word processing programs
- associations of others in your business (They may have sample contracts specific to your industry or trade.)

Have your documents checked by your lawyer before you use them in your business. Getting answers to the questions on the list below makes a good base from which to start in creating your own forms. It also will help you create your own list of information from which an attorney can assist you in drawing up a legal document.

- What is this? agreement, contract, order form?
- Date the agreement was made.
- Date the agreement will be effective.
- How long will it be effective, commencing with the effective date and ending when?
- Definitions of what words mean in the contract, perhaps who or what is meant when the agreement refers to the "buyer," the "product," etc.
- Who are the parties to be named in the contract? (normally you and your customer)
- Purpose: to retain the services or product of _____ for _____.
- Payment method: hourly rates, single fee, fee plus expenses?
- When payments are due: upon receipt, 30 days prior to completion, 30 days after, etc., penalties for late payment, also discount for early payment?
- Exactly what products, services, and duties are all parties expected to perform?
- Completion or delivery date and penalties for late performance?

- Who pays for materials and when?
- Who pays for travel and shipping costs, and when?
- Who will furnish insurance for whom, by what date, and for how long?
- Who is responsible for taxes? Which taxes?
- Who has rights to reproduce the work? Who will own the patent(s)?
- How can the agreement be terminated? On sixty (60) days advance written notice? Verbally? By nonperformance?
- Trade secrets: who do they belong to? Define the use of them by all parties.
- How will disputes be handled? By a court of law? If so, which, when, and how? Or by mediation or arbitration? Again, which, when, and how? For instance, you might state that costs and fees (other than attorneys' fees) associated with the mediation or arbitration shall be shared equally by the parties. Each party shall be responsible for his or her attorney's fees associated with arbitration. Or you might state the other party will need to foot the bill.
- Is it OK to subcontract or hire persons to aid in the work without the prior written consent of the customer?
- How will modifications to this agreement be handled? In writing? Signed by both parties? One? Neither?

Most trouble arises with customers after the agreement has been made and written up. You might agree to do just "some little thing" verbally, but you don't write it down and don't send a copy to your customer. Make sure to at least handwrite the new terms on the old agreement, and put a date with your initials by the changes. Make a copy and fax or mail it to your customer. If you are using a computer, creating a new agreement is easy and quick.

How to Purchase; When to Discontinue

Two of the best—and worst—parts of business are trying to decide what to buy and when to discontinue.

With my life savings of $20,000 we went to New York to begin purchasing materials for my new store. When our purchases came in, everything we had bought fit on our guest room bed. My mama looked at it and was mortified. She knew that I couldn't open a store with inventory that fit nicely on a bed. However, I was luckier than many budding entrepreneurs. She generously gave me another $7,000 to purchase more materials; that gave me a good start at having a decent inventory.

Ron Vandermolen is a hay broker in California. His hobby was collecting old radios of the thirties and forties. This passion soon developed into a cross section of antiques. Soon he was haunting the antique auctions and secondhand stores and finding all kinds of treasures for his home. Before long, friends were asking him to help find items for their homes. He would find just what they wanted and add a slight markup. His friends were thrilled at the bargains they were getting, and Ron was making a profit and doing what he loved best. He rented a small booth at a large antique mall, selling some of his items there. Within that first year he became the mall's number one dealer. One day he met a fellow antique lover, Susan. Before long they were married and together purchased a 1930 California Spanish Revival-style home in southern California, adorned with antiques, of course.

Although Ron still brokers hay, his beloved antique business makes as much income for him as his "real" job. Ron feels he is successful at his business because he listened to his customers and quickly targeted what the most profitable aspects of his business were, in this case, larger pieces and sets of furniture. "It is very important to open your eyes to what is going on around you. Broaden your knowledge to what your customers want."

When something doesn't sell, get rid of it. No matter how much you like it, if your customers don't like it, get it reduced in price until it is gone. If it won't sell at a very low price, give it away for a tax deduction to a charitable group, a Salvation Army or Goodwill thrift store. It is unwise to keep worn-out merchandise or sale merchandise around too long. A bargain basement atmosphere lowers the value of your good merchandise.

The Master Planner

Now listen, you who say, "Today or tomorrow
we will go to this or that city, spend a year there,
carry on business and make money."
Why, you do not even know what
will happen tomorrow. What is your life?
You are a mist that appears for a little while
and then vanishes. Instead, you ought to say,
"If it is the Lord's will, we will live
and do this or that."
—James 4:13–15

No section on planning would be complete without my saying that God is the greatest planner and really the only planner who matters in my life. Even in the matter of publishing this book, God had a different plan. I had approached twenty-three secular publishers to no avail. Then, through a series of circumstances, God opened the door to this publisher, a Christian publisher. The times when my plans have gone awry have been when I have made them myself without seeking his guidance. I certainly believe in having written goals and dreams; however, these are to no avail if God is left out of these plans.

CHAPTER SEVEN

Planning Your Business

Planning for Location, Space, and Equipment

Your hobby business must have two aspects to it: a work space to create your product and an office space to get the business side of your work done. As you create your business spaces, you must find ways to be accessible! Pay attention to those few times your clients mentioned that you're a bit difficult to locate. Most won't even tell you. If even a few do, you have a problem that must be fixed.

Make it easy for your customers to buy! We live in an information age that has many ways to keep you accessible to your customers. If your business takes you on the road, you must get a laptop and a modem. The world no longer waits for you to return to your office to answer their requests. If you cannot be reached, you have lost the opportunity for that business. Respond to every telephone message promptly, within three hours if possible—that way you jump ahead of your competition.

Locating Your Office Space

Do not set up your home office or work space in a hall where there is traffic, near the kitchen with its loud noises, or in the living room where you will disturb your family—and they will disturb you.

Choose a quiet, brightly lit place for all your work. If you do not have a spare bedroom or den to convert into an office or work space, try starting with a corner of a bedroom where you can shut the door, a partitioned section of your garage, or a portion of your basement. Then work toward a separate room for an office or work space as soon as possible.

If possible, choose a room with an outside door and a separate bathroom so your staff can come and go without disturbing the family. If need be, consider converting an appropriate section of your home to accommodate this type of office or work space.

You can save money by purchasing used office furniture and equipment. Check the classified section of your newspaper. Files and desks, which can be refinished, are often available at a Goodwill or Salvation Army store. Often, companies will sell you some of their smaller-sized equipment when they upgrade. Once you start growing, you can replace your used office or work space furniture with new items that reflect your success.

Create a spot that is just for you to create the product or service you intend to sell. You need to treat it with the respect due to a business. It should not be moved "because company is coming to visit." It must become sacred. Once you treat your work and office space with respect, your attitude toward your new business will change.

Only half of your hobby business is the product or service, the other half is the "business." To run a business you need a place from which to run it. One of the enduring images of success in business is to have your own office and staff of employees. Some hobbyists have large office facilities and a number of workers on their payrolls. But the majority run their businesses from their homes.

Working from Home

*Link Resource's 1996 Work-at-Home
Survey found over 34 million people who
work from home in these categories:*

14.9 million people derive their primary
income from self-employment
15.8 a sideline business
7.9 million salaried employees work at
home during normal business hours
—Paul and Sarah Edwards,
speakers and authors of
Working from Home

Working at home has many advantages:

- more time with your family
- far less expense
- often a spouse or older child can become part of the team
- day care need is reduced
- eliminates commuting, parking fees, office rent, and other overhead costs. All you need is a few telephone lines, a mailbox, E-mail, and a fax machine.
- ability to work at odd times without leaving home

Equipping Your Office

There are many possibilities in office equipment and high-tech contraptions. What is vogue or needed today will be passé and outmoded tomorrow. Items listed below are what you should aim at having preferably before you start, but certainly within the first year:

- a computer for your home office with a fax modem
- a laptop computer with a fax modem (that is, if you have a staff at the office and you need to be away from the office for more than a day at a time)
- word processing software
- bookkeeping software
- a dedicated fax machine for incoming faxes
- E-mail system

- on-line access (Internet access and services)
- a business communication system:

  - enough telephone lines (at least three: one for incoming calls, one for the fax, one for your family)
  - voice mail answering system (for your main phone line)
  - pager and/or cellular phone

"But I Don't Know How to Type!"

So learn! Obstacles are those frightful things you see when you take your eyes off your plans. Most kindergarten children know how to use a computer keyboard before they enter school. It's time you do too!

"But my hands are not very dexterous. I could never be a good typist."

When Lilly was eleven years old, she was in an accident and lost most of her left hand. She types about fifty to eighty words per minute using one hand! She personally typed every word in all six of her books.

Do not just sit down and hunt and peck. Get a typing manual or, even better, a typing program for your computer, and learn to "touch type"—typing without looking at the keys. When Lilly was hurt, her mother, Dottie, found out about a special touch-typing system for one-handed people. (You may have read this story in *A Second Helping of Chicken Soup for the Soul* compiled by Jack Canfield and Mark Victor Hansen.)

Today Walters Services sells copies of that old 1955 one-hand touch-typing book in their catalog. Because of Lilly's diligence, she has helped many people who thought typing was difficult or impossible. Lilly is planning to write a modern motivational version of this manual soon herself!

For those of you who are intimidated by computers, buy a simple "learn to type program" from a computer store. It will make the process fun and easy. Introductory computer courses are available from many sources. Check with the nearest community college or your local computer store. Most offer cheap, if not free, computer training. But you will find, as most of us have, that the best way to learn is to just buy a computer and start working.

Although the world is full of suffering,
it is full also of the overcoming of it.
—Helen Keller (1880–1968),
U.S. blind/deaf author, lecturer

What to Do When Your Plans Fail

Failure is only the opportunity to
more intelligently begin again.
—Henry Ford, American businessman,
automobile manufacturer

As an advisor to many individuals who are considering going into business, I am quick to point out that the national business statistic is 85 percent of all new businesses fail. Although that statistic is depressing, it should not be overlooked when deciding whether or not to take the plunge. I think 85 percent of the people in this world just give up too easily. Some of your plans will get fouled up; it's normal. Just don't think of them as failures, think of them as "SNAFU's"—a World War II Army saying, meaning "Situation Normal All Fouled Up." Harriet Beecher Stowe said, "Never give up, for that is just the place and time that the tide will turn."

Meeting Setbacks with GRACE

When you are down and worried, look at your situation with GRACE. I always remind myself of these three sentences when my plans seem to go wrong:

1. God never fails.
2. He is sovereign.
3. He is in control.

As I have said of my quest to walk with GRACE, resilience is one of those important characteristics of success. I don't believe that many things come quickly in the business world. In my life that has certainly been true. Yet I am blessed in many ways. One of my greatest blessings is that both my father and my mother are great heroes to me. Let me elaborate a little.

During the hard times of my business life, especially in the beginning, I would often remember how my father faced difficulties with a GRACE I hope to achieve some day. I never heard him say an unkind thing about another person in all of his eighty-one years. I never heard him complain about having to travel to earn a living or about having to spend most of his life in a hotel room. His noncomplaining spirit was a tribute to his love of God and his influence from his grandfather, the Reverend W. D. Ward.

I went to visit my father in the nursing home after he had many strokes and was unable to walk alone, get up alone, or do anything much for himself. He was frowning a little as if he were in pain. I kissed him and said, "Daddy, do you feel bad?"

Rather than complaining about his very difficult lot in life, he replied, "No, I'm just a little lonely and I'm so glad you have come to see me." Despite his failing health, he only talked about positive things, such as how sweet the nurses were to him and how good and warm his room was in the winter. He looked around under the worst of circumstances and found beauty, joy, and life. He always thanked everyone who came to see him and always asked if we had eaten when his tray was brought to his room. God lived in him and in his actions his whole life. I never saw godly ways more evidenced than I did when he suffered so for the last five years. What a wonderful source of strength he has been in my life. He lived with an attitude of GRACE daily, in the good times and the bad.

My mother is also a hero to me in many ways. She always taught me that we were tough and that we don't quit. She is the epitome of resilience since she always got up when she fell down. She never quit a difficult task and she wouldn't allow us to either. Moral and ethical standards were always kept in my family and she required action of me in all situations. I can hear her saying to me now, "We don't shun responsibility." She never allowed self-pity. She is still great to this day, at age seventy-nine, on figuring out a new plan if Plan A doesn't work.

One of the greatest gifts my mother ever gave to my sister and me was choosing to move herself into an assisted-living apartment when she could no longer live alone without twenty-four-hour help. Her weakness and walking problems, caused primarily by diabetes, got worse and worse. When we approached Mama about considering assisted living, she replied, "I'm one step ahead of you. I've already reserved myself a room in the brand new facility here in Scottsboro. I'm just waiting for it to open."

This was one of the most courageous moves my mother could have taken. Once again, she proved that she was tough and that she wasn't afraid of making difficult decisions without any help from us. I think my sister and I cried more about her leaving her home than she did. She only shed a few tears the last day we were packing her personal belongings to move. She has announced that she loves her new home and that she gets excellent care. The facility really is fabulous and has the most loving and caring staff that I have ever seen. The "girls" who live there have said that it is like living in a sorority house in college again, except for the fact that they all use walkers!

Let us then approach the throne of grace with confidence, so that we may receive mercy and find grace to help us in our time of need.
—Hebrews 4:16

God first: Open your mind to the lessons God is trying to teach you with these setbacks, and you will learn as much or more from these so-called "failures" as from your successes. A college professor was trying to perfect a hearing device so his wife, who was partially deaf, could hear better. He gave all to this passionate dream, and failed. God had another plan for Alexander Graham Bell.

Resilience: If you have made mistakes, there is always another chance for you. You may have a fresh start any moment you choose. Face it with GRACE.

Action: The only place where success comes before work is in a dictionary. We hesitate because we feel inferior. Others take action, make mistakes, and become superior.

Creativity: A seed will only germinate if it dies. Our failures are usually the seeds to our most brilliant successes.

Enthusiasm: "Just buckle in with a bit of a grin."

It Couldn't Be Done

Somebody said it couldn't be done,
but he with a chuckle replied
that "maybe it couldn't ," but he would be one who
wouldn't say so till he'd tried.
So he buckled right in with the trace of a grin
on his face. If he worried he hid it.
He started to sing as he tackled the thing
that couldn't be done, and he did it.
Somebody scoffed: "Oh, you'll never do that;
at least no one ever has done it";
But he took off his coat and he took off his hat,
and the first thing we knew he'd begun it.
With a lift of his chin and a bit of a grin,
without any doubting or quiddit,
he started to sing as he tackled the thing
that couldn't be done and he did it.
There are thousands to tell you it cannot be done
there are thousands to prophesy failure;
there are thousands to point out to you, one by one,
the dangers that wait to assail you.
But just buckle in with a bit of a grin,

just take off your coat and go to it;
Just start to sing as you tackle the thing
that "cannot be done," and you'll do it.
—Edgar A. Guest (1881–1959)

Creating New Plans: Reach for Another Star!

Show me a thoroughly satisfied man
and I will show you a failure.
—Thomas Edison, American inventor

No matter how brilliant your plan may be, facts, years, and experience will introduce a modification, redirection, and oftentimes a disposal. I always reach for another star when the current one is attained. That is part of the fun of business. Notice I said "another star," not "more money." I love the process of creating more products, sharing them worldwide, and making another idea happen. I love meeting new people and sharing the joy of sewing with them. I love seeing new eyes light up as they say, "I just love this type of sewing. It has added a whole new dimension to my life."

My plan in the beginning was simply to have a small retail shop. To help sell in the store, we started teaching classes. Students would buy all of their supplies right there in the store, which greatly increased sales. My plans began to change. Teaching is in my blood. I wanted easier ways to share my knowledge. Suddenly the books and the magazine were born to meet that need. Big seminars grew out of little ones in the store. Now I'm a traveling sewing school and seminar company. When we discovered we still couldn't reach everyone we wanted to touch, we created a television show. Plans change as opportunities arise.

John Amatt lives in a small mountain town in the Canadian Rockies and travels widely to speak. He has addressed more than 500,000 people in thirty countries worldwide on the subject of going "one step beyond." He is the author of the book

Straight to the Top and Beyond: Nine Keys for Meeting the Challenge of Changing Times, published by Jossey-Bass in San Francisco. When John Amatt was a kid growing up in England, his dream was to become a professional adventurer, to make his living from writing and speaking about his expeditions to the highest mountains and most remote places on earth. In those days, such jobs didn't exist, so he had to go out and create his own!

At first, I got a degree in education, which really taught me about effective communication with people. I started out as a school teacher, which gave me the summers off to climb. During that period, I also started a weekly newspaper (learning more about communications) and an outdoor adventure company, guiding people in out-of-the-way places like Greenland and Baffin Island in the Canadian Arctic. Then, having taught for six years at elementary, junior, and senior high, I moved on to adult education, working as an administrator in a management school in the Canadian Rockies.

But all the time, I was climbing mountains and adventuring in exotic places like Nepal, China, and Peru. Then, after two failed attempts to organize international expeditions to climb Mount Everest (at 29,028 feet, the world's highest mountain), I was invited to help head up the first Canadian expedition to Everest in 1982. Knowing this could kick start my career, I wanted to make the climb a high profile event. So I spent two years raising $1 million in sponsorships and establishing a satellite link that would enable us to broadcast live for the first time directly from Everest to North America.

The expedition was an arduous struggle, four of our team died in two tragic accidents early in the climb. But we were able to continue and put six people on top of the world. As a result, we were carried "live" for a month on Canadian national TV news and were featured twice on *ABC Nightline* with Ted Koppel. And my career as a professional adventurer was launched. Along the way, I was constantly learning from my experiences (especially the negative ones) and setting higher goals that would stretch me in their attainment. That's where my company name, "One Step Beyond," came from— the desire to go one step beyond Everest, to take the Everest experience and apply it to the challenges of corporate and professional life.

Why did I succeed? Total focus and dedication to the dream! I always had a clear vision—a mental picture of where I wanted to go. My intuition told me I was moving in the right direction and my desire to prove to myself and others that I could "make it" kept me on track. Many times I was told it was impossible, but this made me all the more determined to prove the doubters wrong.[4]

A man's reach should exceed his grasp,
or what's a heaven for?
—Robert Browning, English poet

Checking New Ideas with a Reality Check

I wish I could tell you I went after all my goals in a smart way. I didn't, and I paid the price many times over. Here is a list of what I should have done before each new venture:

- Decide on the objective of the idea. What is it that you really want to do?
- Tell the others on the team about this objective.
- Forecast the results of this idea if it becomes reality for short-term and long-term in the business.

- Study the resources needed to implement this idea—both people and money.
- Plan alternatives if the idea goes wrong.
- When a decision is made to go ahead with the idea, write details and more details.
- Establish a budget as nearly as you can so surprises won't be crippling.
- Set timetables. Be realistic.
- Choose someone to be project manager. That person will evaluate each step and keep the project on track.
- Is this a course I feel God wants me to travel?

Going from Free to Fee with GRACE

Now you have some ideas to better help you move from free to fee! Always create and recreate your plans with GRACE.

God first in all things: Add God to that "RACE" and you achieve GRACE.

Resilience: Get up when you're down. You conquer by continuing.

> *Let us not become weary in doing good, for at the proper time we will reap a harvest if we do not give up.*
> —Galatians 6:9

Action: It is not enough to dream; wake up and work at it!

> *The heights by great men are reached and kept*
> *Were not attained by sudden flight,*
> *But they, while their companions slept,*
> *Were toiling upwards in the night!*
> —Henry Wadsworth Longfellow
> (1807–1882), U.S. poet

Creativity: Allow the unusual to happen, God gives us no linen, but he does give us flax to spin. Open your mind's eye.

Creativeness often consists of merely turning up what is already there. Did you know that right and left shoes were thought up only a little more than a century ago?
—Bernice Fitz-Gibbon, U.S. advertising executive

Enthusiasm: Allow the spirit of excitement to fill you and spread to your friends. It is contagious and delightfully enriching.

The road to happiness lies in two simple principles: Find what it is that interests you and that you can do well, and when you find it put your whole soul into it— every bit of energy and ambition and ability you have!
—John D. Rockefeller, III, U.S. businessman, entrepreneur

PART 3

THE PROMOTION

Creating Visibility

Dolly Madison, President Madison's wife, was well known for her marvelous public relations at the White House. She always welcomed people with the words "At last!" showing that she was eager to meet them and had been waiting to see them. When her guests left, her departing phrase was "So soon?" letting them know she hated to see them go.

—Dottie and Lilly Walters,
Speak and Grow Rich

CHAPTER EIGHT

What Promotion Can Do for Your Business

It is not enough to build a better mouse trap; you must find all the ways to bring the customers in to look at your mouse trap. All the brilliant customer service, great people skills, and planning don't do you a bit of good until you bring customers in the door! As the word implies, *promotion* is a series of positive actions. I am convinced the most brilliant artists in the world are the unknowns who are sitting at home painting. We never hear about them or buy their work, because they never took the actions to promote their product!

I believe that if one has great service, a great product, an attractive store, a creative advertising plan, great trained employees, and on and on—one has made a good beginning.

Now, who is really going to make it big and stay in business? I believe those who wish to make it in business must decide how to create enough visibility to become a legend. By legend, I believe this is someone who has made a significant contribution in a certain area that brings fulfillment to others' lives. This statement, above all others, expresses my philosophy of business.

To become a legend one must create a plan to make that business

- more creative than all the competition
- more fabulous in service than the industry standard
- more employee friendly to the customers
- more—in every aspect of business!

> *Make no little plans: they have no magic*
> *to stir men's blood.*
> —Daniel H. Burnham (1846–1912),
> U.S. architect and urban planner

Good and even great businesses are a dime a dozen. You must be more than good to keep your doors open year after year. In the hunt of business, your next great catch is just around the corner. Take the actions that bring you around that corner! People say you just need to wait for opportunity to knock on the door. Rubbish! You need to knock on those doors yourself. Find the doors where opportunity is just waiting for you. I keep the attitude in mind that if I can just break into one more market, I will obtain those one hundred more subscriptions to our magazine, and those will open more doors to more and more sales! If I go to speak at one more sewing machine convention, new accounts will emerge and, more importantly, new shops will be excited about heirloom sewing. The hunt for new doors to open is what promotion is about!

Promotion will not increase your bottom line tomorrow. What it will do is

- constantly remind your customers and prospects that you exist and about the benefits of your product or service
- show the world your distinct identity or "personality"
- give you reputation and credibility
- encourage existing customers to buy more
- attract new customers
- replace lost customers.

The Promotional Game Plan

Before you jump in with your checkbook, answer these questions about your promotional efforts:

- What are your overall business plans?
- What is your promotional budget?

- What are the most important features and benefits of your product/service?
- Who is your target audience?
- Who is your competition?
- How does the world perceive your business relative to your competition?
- What personality or business culture do you want to project?
- What is the single most important benefit you want to convey about your product/service?
- What other benefits set you apart from the competition?
- How will you measure the effectiveness of your promotional programs?

Some Promotional Ideas

Advertising people tell me you need to expose your customers to your product nine times before they are apt to buy. The hard part is promoting your business without spending any money, or spending as little as possible. Most small businesses can't afford much advertising. Here are more than seventy promotion ideas, some free, some inexpensive, a few costly. All will give your business exposure.

Some items below will receive a fuller explanation later in Part 3. Others are self-explanatory.

- Get out there and do something. Better to do something for nothing than nothing for nothing.
- Get out and get among 'em!
- Ask for referrals.
- Look for new ways to make contact with customers.
- Keep in touch.
- Target your market!
- Create a promotional plan.
- Set dates for when you will accomplish the items on your plan.

- Create a logo.
- Create a mission.
- Create a letterhead.
- Create matching business cards.
- Create a great flyer.
- Send flyers and special offers with promo along with billing statements.
- Be smart with your advertising dollar.
- Go after word-of-mouth advertising.
- Do a display in the window at your local library.
- Create a presentation/press kit. (These include flyers, articles by or about you, photos, brochures, product samples, anything interesting about you.)
- Put flyers up in your supermarkets, laundromats, pet stores—anywhere your customers like to frequent.
- Send press releases to the media about your product or service.
- Create contests or sweepstakes.
- Take surveys.
- Leave a trail of "gifts" back to you.
- Trade your product or service for publicity.
- Co-op with your suppliers for ads.
- Write articles for newsletters and magazines.
- Create a Web page.
- Post information articles on your Web site and allow people to reprint them in their trade publications and company newsletters.
- Get the media to write and talk about you!
- Get great photos!
- Create a mailing list.
- Create your own newsletter and send to your mailing list.
- Create your own E-mail newsletter.
- Do desktop marketing via the Internet.
- Give speeches to civic and service clubs and groups (Kiwanis, PTAs, Chamber of Commerce, etc.).
- Give free promotional seminars.

- Give demonstrations of your hobby at trade shows, craft shows, and any event happening in your community.
- Team up with other hobbyists for promotions and advertising.
- Start associations and users' groups.
- Create a forum or newsgroup on the Internet.
- Always carry and give out your business cards.
- Always get potential customers' business cards or write down their information when you meet them.
- Imprint your company name and logo on giveaway items for your customers:
  - pens
  - paper
  - clocks
  - calendars
- Give funny bumper stickers.
- Put your message on:
  - shopping store receipts
  - shopping bags
  - your own cars
  - your team's cars
  - billboards
  - bus stop benches,
  - inside buses and subways
  - vehicle and building signs
  - point-of-sale displays
- Cosponsor events with nonprofit organizations and advertise your participation.
- Co-op events with related, yet noncompeting, businesses.
- Cosponsor events with your suppliers.
- At consumer or business trade shows you could:
  - attend
  - have a display booth
  - give educational mini-seminars
- Do telemarketing.
- Train everyone on your team, including your young family members, to be service and salespeople.

- Become involved in your community.
- Create gift certificates.
- Promote your business with GRACE: with God first in all things, Resilience, Action, Creativity, and Enthusiasm.

Your promotional ideas will only be limited by the time and creativity you give to thinking of them. Whatever strategies you use to get your name out into the public, make sure something in it leads back to you. If you write an article, make sure you find a way to mention your location, e.g., "Here in Huntsville, Alabama, we have a . . ." or "Just like our local Little League, the Huntsville Alabama Tiger's, did the other day when . . ." If you give anything away as a promo, make sure it has a lead that will point the way back to you. If you get involved in your community, have your company be the sponsor so your name is emblazoned in your potential customers' minds. These become constant beacons in the community, saying, "Look over here!"

Do Something for Nothing

Patricia Fripp, professional speaker, says in her talks, "It is better to do something for nothing, than nothing for nothing." Don't sit around and wait for business to come in. In starting what would later be a very successful beauty salon, Patricia would grab people off the street when she didn't have customers and give them a free haircut! Of course they went away talking about her business.

Lilly's hobby is singing. She wanted to find a way to make it pay. She got three of her friends and created a Dickens caroling group. Creating business cards and sending out faxes to businesses in the area got them a few bookings. What really brought in the customers was walking up and down the street in full costume at their local village street fair singing the old Christmas tunes. After each song they would say to the crowd, "We are the Holiday Traditions! We do corporate and private parties, and we

would love to do yours!" Now each December is full of bookings for their little group.

Get Out and Get Among 'Em

Get out there and see what others in your field are doing and
saying. Don't just hang out with the other beginners, find people
who are doing what you hope to be doing someday. Watch what
they do, and emulate it. Getting out, networking, and learning
are brilliant tools to promote your business and bring customers
to you. Others will see that you are "in motion" and will begin to
refer business to you.

Barbara Pachter's passion was photography. She was teaching elementary school, but she used all her extra time and
money to learn about the "profession" of photography. She set
up a darkroom in her house, took courses, read everything on
the subject, attended professional meetings, talked to other
photographers, and found a mentor. "I was obsessed with
learning everything I could to become skilled in the profession." When an opening for a freelancer appeared at a small
local newspaper, she was recommended by someone in her
new network of photography friends for the job. She received
five dollars for each picture used. Eventually she became the
first female photographer at the *Philadelphia Bulletin*, a large
paper that sent her on assignments to the Super Bowl and the
Democratic National Convention.

The Best Way to Get Referrals

Oh, those glorious referrals! Referrals help to prequalify the
population and get you in front of more interested people in less
time with the least amount of expense.

If I tell a new dealer prospect what we charge for one of our
seminars, he or she will probably gulp and think, *Nobody can
charge per day what she does!* But when a dealer we have done
a seminar for in the past tells the prospect about the income we

generated for their store, suddenly we become very believable. Our best referral system is having satisfied customers.

Recently while I was teaching in Florida I had the chance to have lunch with a young lady of seventy-four years who was still making wedding and bridesmaid dresses. She shared how she purchased an electric sewing machine when she was a young bride. She only had the money to purchase a treadle machine which cost ten dollars. The electric machine cost much more—a grand total of $110. The salesman left her a treadle machine as well as the spectacular electric machine with a challenge: "Christi, if you refer me to leads where I sell an electric machine, I will give you a credit toward your ten dollars per month payment on this electric machine. I think I can help you earn your machine." From that day on, Christi began to ask friends who would like to see a demonstration on this marvelous new invention, the electric sewing machine. She was able to refer enough leads to him that he faithfully paid her ten-dollar payment for enough months to pay out her machine.

The absolute best way to get referrals is first by doing a good job for a customer and second by asking for them. You ask for them by way of networking. I'm not talking about the stereotypical form of networking where a person hands out his or her business card to everyone they meet, slaps people on the back, and obnoxiously says, "Hey, let's do lunch." I'm talking about cultivating relationships.

Ways to Encourage Referrals

Set your mind to it, and you will begin to see many proactive ways to get referrals. The best time to get referrals is when the customer has just made a happy purchase. Try some of these ways to encourage referrals:

- Simply *ask* your current customers and prospects for:
  - a referral letter to be included in your satisfied customer book

- actual names for you to call using their name as a referral
- names—if they result in a sale, give your customers some type of commission
- Ways to ask:
  - "Can you think of someone else who might benefit from this?"
  - "Can you suggest other organizations I might contact? Do you know anyone at that organization?"
  - "I am interested in working with the XYZ company (or organization). Do you know anyone there?"
- Give each customer something to encourage a return visit, perhaps a "2 for 1" or a 15-percent-off coupon.
- After getting referral names, call the prospective customer with the opening that mentions the person who suggested you call, "Judy Masters has suggested that I call you."
- Never be too busy to send a thank-you to the referring person! If you don't thank them, they won't send referrals to you any more! Being "too busy" to thank people who take care of your business probably means that you won't have much of a business left in the near future.
- The best way to get business and get referrals is to give business and give referrals. Ask people what you can do to help them. Help them make connections to what their needs and dreams are. Add a postscript to your conversations (and thank-you notes), asking how you can be on the lookout for business for them. Be noticed for how much you give—not what you want.
- Plant seeds of suggestion in your customers' minds, like "My clients tend to refer me to others. . . ." and "I'm so blessed. Most of my work comes through referrals."
- You will have the greatest chance of success if you can get the other person to introduce you to their referrals. That way, when you call or mail, the prospect already expects you and is more willing to receive your call. If

your phone allows conference calls, you can ask them to hang on while you conference it right then.

Think of New Ways to Make Contact

Keep in touch with your clients through newsletters, E-mail, postcards, and the like. Prospects who are often approached by those hoping to sell them something can get very tired of being approached. Work on creative ways to say hello. Send a cardboard box with two helium balloons inside. The balloons might say, "Have a great day," or "Just to say hello." Tied to the ribbons on the bottom, say, "Jack Helms gave me your name as someone whom I would really like to meet. Let me introduce myself and I'd like to call for an appointment."

Target Your Market: Plant in the Good Ground

Promotion that tries to reach everyone rarely succeeds. When you target your efforts within a specific market, several good things will happen for you:

- You gain expertise to better serve your customers.
- Current customers talk about you to others, and referrals start to pour in.
- You gain a reputation as an expert (experts are sought after).
- Doing your work is easier.
- Your business grows in volume and profitability.

Think of those who will be most interested in your product. Target your promotional efforts with a specific customer in mind. Targeting might be done to almost any criteria, but these are the most common:

- Demographics: gender, age, income, location of residence or business, etc.
- Behaviors: the products, services, or vendors they currently use; their current level of awareness of your type of business; how often they buy your type of product or service, etc.

- Wants, needs, and desires: What benefits currently attract your potential customers? Upon what basis will they decide whether to use your type of product or service? Does your business fulfill those wants, needs, and desires, etc.?

Listen! A farmer went out to sow his seed. As he was scattering the seed, some fell along the path, and the birds came and ate it up. Some fell on rocky places, where it did not have much soil. It sprang up quickly, because the soil was shallow. But when the sun came up, the plants were scorched, and they withered because they had no root. Other seed fell among thorns, which grew up and choked the plants, so that they did not bear grain. Still other seed fell on good soil. It came up, grew and produced a crop, multiplying thirty, sixty, or even a hundred times.
—Mark 4:3–8

Promotional Tools

To promote your business, you need the most basic of marketing tools:

- mailing lists
- business cards—in any field a business card is required. On your card include your main area of expertise and, of course, all the information on how to locate you.
- letterhead—a sheet of writing paper bearing as the heading your name, your company name, and what you do. Create your letterhead to match your business cards and flyers or materials. Many of your promotional items—price list, schedules, flyers—can be reproduced on your letterhead for a professional look.
- flyers
- giveaway items
- photos
- press releases and articles

How to Develop a Mailing List

It is not so much what you mail, as to whom you mail it that will bring you business. Even the best mailing piece is "junk mail" if you send it to the wrong person. Whenever you get a sale or an inquiry, keep the data! Your business is not your product or service; your database of prospects and customers is your business.

My first mailing was to shops that had bought something from me already. That inaugural mailing list was hand-printed on a piece of paper. When I wanted to do a mailing, I simply took this list to the photocopy shop and they photocopied it onto mailing labels.

You will create your mailing list from those you personally meet, work with, and sell to, and from lists you buy from many sources. When you buy a list from someone else, the best way to insure the quality of a list is to find out how and when it was generated. The people who buy one type of product from you or a company like yours are great prospects for new business.

You may also want to consider finding others with similar but noncompetitive businesses who may be willing to trade lists with you. You might even do a team mailing to promote your business and split the costs of printing and postage.

Those who have bought from you personally, and have had a good experience, are your main source of future sales. Always keep track of them in a database. Remember, when networking it is much more important to get cards from people than it is to give yours, so you can add them to your database.

Wally Crowder, a professional stuntman, loved to "play" on his computer. Being a second unit director and stunt coordinator for the film industry, he came up with the idea to log the nation's stunt men and women. He took all the names that he had in his computer and did a mailing that brought in 450 applicants at fifty dollars per person. That was the first Stunt Players Directory. He began to generate income by selling advertisements in the back of the directory. As of the last directory, he has enlisted more than one thousand applicants with the publication. It is published by Wally and his wife, Lori, in a small office in the backyard. They have now taken all of the stunt people in the directory and put them on the Internet worldwide as a part of the Stunt Directory On-Line.

In the old days we kept our leads on a 3x5 card system. Today, computers are so inexpensive and easy to learn, it does not make any sense to try to keep your database on paper. Your database/mailing list should include at least the following information on your prospects:

- first and last name
- address, city, state, zip
- phone and fax number
- E-mail address
- what they purchased from you
- what their special interests are in your product or service

From all of that information, your database manager software will be able to create other mailing lists—for instance, a fax list, or an E-mail list, which are much less expensive to send than "snail mail" (traditional post mail).

Flyers to Promote Your Classes, Products, and Services

A flyer will be one of the most important items you will need for the first several years in promoting your business. It should be a simple one-sided sheet. Your flyer should tell your customers the following:

- What you are selling: seminars? books? dog grooming? This goes at the top of the page and should be small. What is to be emphasized is the benefit of what you are selling, like "Chemical-Free Dog Grooming."
- Title of business or classes: very bold and large, this should stand out.

- What is covered: (short outline and/or bullet points) this gives them an idea of the content. If giving classes, begin this section with "You Will Learn . . ."
- Who this is most appropriate for: Buyers want stuff that is specific for them. If you are a dog trainer, you are more apt to buy an answering machine that is just for dog trainers, even though it is really not different than other answering machines. Indicate if your products are best for housewives, Ph.Ds, dog lovers, managers, salespeople, front line personnel, etc. If you say your items are appropriate for all, all will think you don't know what you are talking about, even if you are right.
- A few endorsements: These show you are liked by other customers.
- A very short biography: It tells why you are an expert on this subject.
- What you look like: Your photograph or a drawing of you.

Make your flyers faxable! In today's cyber-fast world, customers want information now! That means making your flyers faxable. Have you ever been faxed something from a magazine, perhaps a page with a bit of color on it? It is a solid black mess when it arrives. So why not design your flyers so they will look good when they arrive at their destination? As you create new materials, just fax them to yourself to make sure they look nice on the other end.

Here are a few tips to make your materials faxable:

- Use white paper with black or a very dark ink. Remember, all colors reproduce at the receiver's end as white or black. Any backgrounds or colored paper may make your whole fax a big black blob.
- Do not use large areas of black; these take a *long* time to fax.
- Avoid photos; consider having an artist do a line drawing of you.

Promotional Gifts

Many small businesses create unusual gifts to give their customers and potential customers. This type of gift should be something that can be shared with staff. Your gift should never be embarrassing, crude, personal, or anything that could be considered a bribe.

If you use gifts, keep them fun, inexpensive, and practical! Useable items are kept around. We have sent out soda can covers, key chains, and letter openers with good response. If your business is a "how-to" business, you might send an instructional sheet for a new design. That is much less expensive than plastic goodies from the promotional catalog.

Publicity Releases

Once you have a database of press contacts, you need to work your list. This is done by periodically calling and sending your contacts publicity releases. Publicity releases are short news accounts that you will send to the news media for anything you conceive of that might have a "hook."

There are thousands of PR companies that will help you create and send out press releases, but this is very expensive. On the other hand, it is the easiest way to accomplish getting your name in front of the press. The least expensive and fastest way to send releases is from your own computer. You just take your database and create a fax phone book (instructions to do this come with every fax modem). Your computer then sends the releases to whomever you wish, usually in the middle of the night when the rates are less expensive.

Rules for News Releases

If you follow these rules, the media will pay closer attention to your news release and work with you:

1. Put the source of the release in the upper left-hand corner of your paper. This is the name, address, and phone

number of the person to contact for further information. The contact person may be you or someone at your PR service.

2. Put the release date, typed in capital letters, slightly below the source information and on the opposite (right-hand) side of the page.

3. Sum up the most important thrust of the release in the headline in capital letters.

4. Use standard 8 1/2 x 11 sheets of paper. Smaller or larger sizes are hard for media people to store. Use only one side of the paper. Keep the length of the release to one page whenever possible. If you must use more, type "(MORE)" at the bottom. Staple all pages on top left. On the last page, type "###" or "END."

5. Your releases should be typed double-spaced. Leave a three-inch margin on the top of the first page and leave margins on each side that are wide enough for editing.

6. Dottie Walters' journalism teacher wrote the following poem by Rudyard Kipling on the blackboard the first day Dottie was in her class. It has since helped her in every business enterprise.

"I keep six honest serving men, They taught me all I knew. Their names were What and Where and When, And How and Why and Who."

Be sure to get all of your "serving men" in the first paragraph of your news releases. Put the most important and exciting one at the head of the story.

7. Use a fine grade of paper. A color other than white may help you stand out in the crowd but stay in the warm spectrum.

8. Don't send out news releases that have a "copy machine" look.

9. Avoid highly technical language unless the release is for a technical audience.

10. Find out how far in advance each contact wants your information. Send it out when they want it.

11. Don't pass off nonoriginal material as exclusive.

12. Don't try to make an advertisement for yourself out of an article or release. Make it fascinating news for readers instead.

13. Give a source for additional information (name, address, phone number). Make sure your source knows all the details and does not have to check with someone else for answers if a reporter calls for additional information. This source could be an association or company mentioned in the article.

14. Find a way to make your news noteworthy! Give it a twist that is specific to the audience who will read it. A dog expert working with plumbers might come up with a topic such as "Plumbers Use Dogs to Sniff Out Deadly Gas" to catch the attention of a plumbers' publication. Other news media outlets, however, might also find that topic worthy of attention.

15. Releases should be the minimum length necessary to present the facts of interest to this audience.

16. Keep your news release mailing list up-to-date. Post changes as you receive them. Media people like to see releases addressed to them rather than to their predecessors.[5]

Get Those Photos!

Newspapers are very keen to print great photos. If you can supply them with a great black and white photo, in a timely manner (usually twelve hours after the event), they will very often print them. If you have someone affiliated with you—a student, parent, friend—who likes to take pictures, you will be well ahead of the game! After the event, take the film immediately to a quality developer and take the best shots to your local papers. They really love to print good shots with a short mention of what you are doing.

Magazines are more picky. They want great color shots. You will need a professional for that type of photo.

Magazines and newspapers want either black and white or color photos, or electronic versions of photos. As newspapers and magazines inquire about you, you will need good publicity shots on hand in batches of at least fifty each, which is very costly if you use actual glossy photos. Instead, you can get economical reproductions at any copy center. Instead of sending glossy photos for "just inquiries," send out a copy on regular paper. (Double check before doing this to insure your photographer does not have restrictions on copying the photo. Some may, and copying would be a copyright infringement.) You can use your computer to create labels that say "glossy photo available upon request." This lets the media know you have real glossy photo prints of the original if they like them.

PR Is Essential

In conclusion, public relations and publicity are necessary events in a successful business. Use a little creativity and the ideas gleaned from this chapter and you will have a good start.

I have never been able to afford an advertising agency, so we have had to be very creative. A few phone calls to newspapers and television stations have opened the doors to getting publicity for my business. In my husband's dental practice, a phone call or two have brought the medical editor out to see what news was happening in implant dentistry, new equipment, or missionary dentistry around the world. All of these phone calls developed into stories in the newspaper.

Never give up on looking for ways to get free or affordable publicity. It is essential.

CHAPTER NINE

Be Smart with Your Advertising Dollar

I knew absolutely nothing about advertising nationally. I soon found out that it was quite expensive, yet I felt I needed the exposure. The good news is, unlike other promotional efforts, when you are paying for it, you have the final word in determining where, when, and how often your message will appear, how it will look, and what it will say.

The objective of all advertising efforts is obvious: to inform and persuade customers to buy. What advertising cannot do is create an instant sharp increase in sales, solve cash flow problems, or substitute for bad customer service or products. What advertising can do is act as one of many promotional tools you can, and should, use to draw in more customers. It gives you one more exposure to your potential market. People don't see every one of your promotional efforts. They only see some of them, some of the time. It's constant repetition and the cumulative effect that bring customers to you.

Advertising works best and costs least when planned and targeted carefully in advance. Preplanning gives you the benefit of paying less per ad in most publications by agreeing to run several ads over time rather than deciding issue by issue.

What Do You Want Your Advertising to Accomplish?

Everyone wants advertising to bring hundreds of customers stampeding through the door. Sometimes it does, but for your advertising plan to work it requires you to be more precise. Set specific advertising goals. Yours might be to

- attract new customers
- attract your competitors' customers

- create immediate sales
- create immediate sales leads
- enhance the image of your business
- get the customer to call with questions
- produce awareness of your business
- develop current customer loyalty
- upsize each order
- promote special events

What Should Your Advertising Say?

Advertisements use words, images, or sounds that are alluring and yet informational. To be effective, advertising *must* include

- a message that will clearly call out to your target customer that something important is waiting for them
- explanation of the important benefits
- something that grabs and keeps their attention and interest
- something that motivates them to take some action
- something that makes it easy for customers to respond

To be effective, advertising might include

- emphasis of the most desirable benefits of the product or service—perhaps convenience, style, or durability
- comparisons with competitive products, two-for-one sales, special one-day discounts, offers of free information
- focus on a single idea—perhaps a special offer, new price, features, quality, or a convenience. Your entire ad then supports this single idea.
- adding drama to the most mundane of topics. Deal with your use of drama in your advertising with GRACE.

To stimulate your thinking, collect your successful competitors' advertising materials. Also pick up the materials of others that sell to the same market you want to reach. This will help you see what is working with your targeted audience.

"FREE with Purchase" Works Magic

When you offer something special with the purchase, you have a tried-and-true method of increasing sales. Just keep it easy and simple to produce from your end. Several years ago my son and I were searching desperately for a way to increase the subscription base to our magazine, *Sew Beautiful*. We had tried several FREE ideas, including three yards of free lace mailed to all subscribers. Needless to say, it was a lot of trouble to cut three yards of lace! Instead we found a free instructional video to be effective; it raised our subscription base 30 percent and has been so effective we have used it for the past five years.

A man with a video rental store in an area with many competitors wondered what he could offer to those who rented videos from him. All the stores had the same movies. He thought: "What goes well with movies? Popcorn!"

His wife made the best caramel popcorn you ever tasted. So, he had her make up a big batch of these balls, wrapped them in Saran Wrap, and handed one out with every rental. Soon his store was jammed! People loved the caramel corn so much he then marketed it to be sold in grocery and specialty stores, and created a whole new business.

—Dottie and Lilly Walters,
*101 Simple Things to Grow
Your Business and Yourself*

Evaluating Media to Fit Your Needs

Really knowing your audience, knowing what they like, dislike, and in this case what media they listen to or read, will guide you to where you will want to advertise. What works well for some types of products or services may be totally ineffective for others.

My first advertising was in a trade journal. It reached the audience we needed to contact and was much less expensive than other options. Over the years, I found by painful and expensive mistakes what works and what does not work for my business. Now I make fewer mistakes in choosing the media in which I advertise because I follow these strategies that I am suggesting to you. Look for media that

- fit your advertising goals
- reach your target market efficiently
- reach your target geographical area
- are within your advertising budget
- are a good value—the cost is relative to the number of people they reach

Types of Media

There are as many types of media for you to advertise in as there are ideas in the universe. Every month even more new advertising options become available. Beyond "traditional" media—television, radio, newspapers, magazines, outdoor billboards, direct mail, and the Yellow Pages—open your mind to other places for paid advertisements:

- the Web
- newsletters
- journals
- local cable television
- airport boards
- ski lift boards
- television monitors in the front of grocery carts
- advertising card packs that come in the mail

The following summarizes the advantages and disadvantages of the more traditional advertising media:

Television

Television provides a means for reaching a great number of people in a short period of time. The number of target audience who see your ad depends upon how many viewers are tuned in to the television station at a specific time. Television is wonderful in that it gets your message to your potential customers with sight, sound, and motion. On the other hand, it has a much higher cost for a rather short airtime.

Small businesses will typically use either spot television or cable television. A spot television ad is placed on one station in one market. Cable is a much less expensive alternative to broadcast television advertising. Of course, your audience is much smaller, depending upon the cable viewership in a given market.

Radio

Airtime and production costs are much less in radio advertising, making it relatively inexpensive. Even though there is no visual, your message will still quickly reach a large number of potential customers. Also, there are so many radio program formats that it is easy to sensibly target your audience.

Newspapers

One of the nice things about newspaper ads, compared to radio or TV, is you have the possibility of the reader's keeping the newspaper for later reference. A customer can be exposed to your ad many times, giving your ad a longer life. With radio and TV, all kinds of distractions might take your listener's mind away from your message when it airs. But in newspapers, readers take their time with your message, hopefully coming back to your ad if they get distracted. Newspapers also reach a large number of people within a specified geographic area.

Magazines

Unlike newspapers, magazines have pass-along value and excellent quality of production. Before a magazine is discarded it is often looked through several times and often by several people. This gives magazines a relatively longer ad life and repeated ad exposure. By their nature, they have a highly targeted audience for consumer and business readers. More so than newspapers, they focus on geographic area, demographics, or lifestyle. The disadvantages of magazines are long lead time, higher costs in production, and ad price.

Outdoor (Billboards)

Outdoor advertising helps you completely cover a geographic area with high levels of viewing frequency. Billboard ads are not normally used on their own but as a reinforcement of other advertisements and promotions. The advantages of billboards are that they are well seen. On the other hand, the viewer does not get much time with a billboard because the reader is usually moving. To get your message across you must keep the message simple, brief, and easily understood at a glance.

Yellow Pages

Yellow Pages ads have "permanence." Your customer will usually keep several phone books around as a regular reference. So when your customers are ready to "take action," you are there. They also allow you to target a geographic area. Ads here are relatively low in cost. However, ads can be changed only once per year, so it is not a "timely" method of advertising.

Find What Media Your Customers Frequent

Finding what media your customers actually read is simple. Just ask them! Whenever someone calls in or comes in the door, find a quick way to ask them a few questions. The SBA provides the questionnaire below for your use, with twelve questions. I prefer to use only three or four. The shorter it is, the better your chances for getting it filled out. But this will provide a good base to build a questionnaire appropriate to your business.

1. How did you first hear about us?
2. Have you seen any of our advertising? If so, where?
3. What do you like best/find most useful about our product/service?
4. How could our product/service be improved?

5. What other products/services would you like us to offer?
6. What was the single most compelling reason for choosing our product/service?
7. What other reasons were important?
8. What friends, family members, or colleagues, if any, influenced your buying decision?
9. What newspapers and magazines do you read regularly?
10. Which radio and television stations do you tune in most frequently?
11. Please indicate your age and sex:
    ( ) Male ( ) Female ( ) 18-34 ( ) 35-49
    ( ) 50-65 ( ) 66+
12. Please indicate your annual household income:
    ( ) Under $15,000 ( ) $16-24,000
    ( ) $25-49,000 ( ) $50-100,000 ( ) $100,000+
    (For businesses, omit #11 and instead ask something to indicate size, such as number of employees. Rather than #12, ask for annual sales volume.)

Other Advertising Strategies

Trade Your Product or Service for Publicity

You may find many magazines, newsletters, even radio or television stations that would be willing to exchange your product or service in return for free advertising. Keep your mind open for opportunities to barter. Larger publications are not as keen to barter, but many small radio stations, newspapers, magazines, and newsletters are willing.

Before you barter, make sure their readership/listenership is part of your target market. (Be sure to talk to a tax specialist about the appropriate way for you to report barter on your tax forms in your own situation.) Even if the audience is not just right for what you do now, how about creating other products? These ads can bring you cash sales. An ad is a concrete value that has a price with which you can negotiate.

Note: Trade should be taken at least in full dollar-to-dollar retail value of the item or even more. The markup on items the client barters is often 75 percent over the wholesale cost. Exchange your normal "listed" full fee/price for their full retail list price on their items. Both of you will receive a bargain.

Team Up with Other Hobbyists to Promote Yourself

Team up to buy a joint ad, Web site, or share use of a toll-free, wide-area telephone number (800-number), or any type of advertisement with other hobbyists. Since advertising is often expensive, consider sharing a full-page ad with others in your field.

Try to find those not in direct competition with you, but who compliment what you do. If you make frames, find someone who sells paint. If you do smocking, find someone who does quilting, etc.

Co-op Advertising Programs

Remember, you can stretch your media budget by taking advantage of co-op advertising programs offered by manufacturers to encourage you to advertise their products. Although programs vary, generally the manufacturer will pay for a portion of media space and time costs or mailer production charges, up to a fixed amount per year. The total amount contributed is usually based on the quantity of merchandise you purchase.

How to Get More Information on Advertising

- Small Business Administration (800)-8-ASK-SBA
- Television Bureau of Advertising, Inc. (212) 486-1111
- Radio Advertising Bureau, Inc. (212) 254-4800
- Newspaper Advertising Bureau (212) 921-5080
- Magazine Publishers of America (212) 752-0055
- Outdoor Advertising Assoc. of America (202) 371-5566
- Direct Marketing Association (212) 768-7277
- Yellow Pages Publishers Association (313) 680-8880

CHAPTER TEN

Using Trade Shows, Associations, Catalogs, and Media

How I Became a "Legend" in My Own Industry

Promotion is far more than just flyers or even articles and interviews in the media. The following were several promotional strategies that set us apart in my own industry:

- writing books and more books
- developing an international magazine
- developing a television series for PBS
- teaching all over the world
- expanding into new, yet related, industries, such as the doll and teddy bear dressing industry
- newsletter and mailing list creativity
- conducting free one-hour classes in a retail store
- Christmas in July
- in-shop demonstrations
- contests and drawings (for drawings, make it clear that anyone can register—no purchase necessary)
- programs for civic clubs
- educational programs
- Christmas cards
- thank-you letters

Become the Industry Standard

Do you call a copy machine a Xerox? Do you call a cotton swab a Q-Tip? Do you call a soda a Coke? These companies came along and set such a standard that we all think of the entire industry in their terms.

Think about how you might set the standard in your business. What are you going to do to be different? What are you going to do to be better?

Competition is a wonderful thing. It makes the business world go round and round and sometimes upside down. In my business I decided to become the industry standard by writing better sewing books, using more beautiful art, writing instructions that were clearer, printing more color pictures, and creating something that would be a wonderful value for the dollar charged. That wasn't too hard to do. We just worked harder, added more pages to our books, and traveled to more shows to show our goods.

Developing a Good Reputation in the Business and Private Community

I have a philosophy of business volunteer work. All the large companies are very philanthropic. Why can't small businesses be involved in volunteer work also? It will probably bring more free publicity to your business than you could afford to pay for with your limited advertising budget. There are many ways to contribute to charity in your area. Consider these that will also promote your business:

- Benefit shows/events for charity: Create a show or event based on your hobby, and give the profits to a charity in your area. You will get great press, great PR, and a great sense of GRACE.
- How-to slide shows: For civic groups to help with their education.

- Speaking for civic groups: Speaking for free, with a topic that will let others know what you do, yet be of great benefit to them, creates a wonderful win/win relationship.

Trade and Consumer Shows

Trade and consumer shows can be an excellent way to sell your product. From antiques to teddy bears to stamps, from wood carvings to the painted items, from baseball cards and toys to art, a craft show is one of the best for any type of business that is hobby-related. People love craft shows, flea markets, and other types of booth trade shows.

Al Peterson uses trade shows as one method to make his hobby pay. He says it has helped him find a way to do what he loves best in a way that is at least self-supporting. As he says, "At least I have made my lifestyle tax deductible! I actually combined three or maybe four hobbies into my business—stamp collecting, model railroading, railroad history, and train watching. This weekend will be the perfect example. I am doing the Hostler's Model Railroad Show in Ogden, Utah. It is held in the historic Union Station—a beautiful building with large wooden ceiling beams and murals depicting the building of the transcontinental railroad. At my table, I will sell train stamps, railroad event and railway post office covers, railroad advertising labels, train and depot postcards, old prototype and model magazines, railroad stock certificates, and other paper railroad memorabilia. I'll revel in the camaraderie of meeting and talking with other people with interests like mine and sharing their stories and experiences. Plus I'll have operating model train layouts across the aisle to watch throughout the show and an occasional real train to watch through the window behind me. This is my idea of heaven and I get to live it almost every weekend. I think my key to success is enthusiasm—when you love what you are doing, that comes across in everything you do and it's contagious. I go to stamp shows to inform stamp collectors about the joys of trains and railroading, and I go to train shows to educate rail enthusiasts about all the historic paper memorabilia. I put out a monthly newsletter that includes some of my biography and philosophy (along with useful information)." You can read his newsletters and get other information from his Web site at http://www.collectors-mall.com/trp/trp.htm.

Tips Before You Go to a Show

- Going to craft shows is an excellent way to have custom garments or custom furniture or custom photography on display for people to see. You might not have anything to sell at the first few shows but rather just take orders. This is a wonderful way for lots of new people to see the type of work you do.

- Create pleasing business cards and a brochure to hand out. Include on this the length of time that should be expected before delivery.

- Also be very specific about your terms and payment. I suggest that you get at least three-fourths of the total charge before the work is begun. Have a legal contract for the people to sign before you begin your work unless you are sure that you can sell the product to someone else. Many people who make custom products simply require all payment up front. This is simplest if you can do it.

- Choose the best craft shows in your area. To find out which is best, call your local crafts people or go by stores and ask if they know of any consumer shows that are well attended. Ask your friends who enjoy the craft. Contact the chamber of commerce concerning all the shows in your area. Contact organizations to see if booths are available. Rent a booth.

- Start with a small booth or table space unless the space is very inexpensive. I believe that it is better to try several shows in a small space and see which ones are most profitable rather than to spend all of your money on a big booth at the first show you try.

- Some shows are hard to get into; some are not. The earlier you call to reserve booth space, the better. Ask the organization people if any of their better booths are available. If the top spots are not available, request the best remaining booth. A few organizations are so large that you have to get on a waiting list, which could be forever. Most, however, have plenty of space with each show.

Important Secrets to Selling at a Show

How do you sell lots at a show even when everybody else is griping that "nobody came to this show"? We have sold at shows with a very low attendance and set almost record sales. Here are some of the rules for having a successful show.

Don't Ever Say "May I Help You?"

Don't ever say "May I help you?" to passersby. This is the world's worst greeting for a sales situation. The automatic answer is "No, thanks, I'm just looking." What people really feel is "I need to get out of here because someone is pushing themselves on me."

What should you say? "How are you this morning?" is a good starter. If the booth is very busy and kind of crazy, you might say, "Welcome to the world of insanity." Everybody laughs when you openly recognize that the place is a bit busy. Here are some other inviting comments to encourage people to stay and look for awhile.

- "I'd like to invite you in to look at everything in the booth."
- "You have a beautiful baby."
- "Your little girl has the most beautiful eyes." (Everybody in the world has beautiful eyes; just begin to notice.)
- "Are you having a good time at the show?"
- "It looks like you have already bought the whole show out."

- "Please feel free to come in and look at and touch everything in this booth."
- "Would you like to sit down for a little while in our booth chair? It looks to me like you are tired."
- "I really like your outfit."

Dress Appropriately

My employees wear "church clothes" or dressy casual clothes in the booth, usually with new and clean-looking athletic shoes or comfort shoes. I have found you need to be comfortable to be charming to customers. I have been to shows where the dealers' clothing was dirty, their hair was dirty, they smelled bad, and they had worn-out blue jeans or completely unstylish clothing. Remember, you have about five seconds to be pleasing enough to invite your customers to enter your booth. An inviting appearance goes a long way!

Stand on Your Feet and Smile

Joy is easy to spread, and a big beautiful smile is probably the best way to do this task. Smile at everybody who comes by and say a little pleasantry, such as, "It seems as if you have shopped until you dropped." Smile at all of your customers while they are in the booth. Seem happy and have a natural laugh.

Only if there are no customers on the floor should "booth etiquette" and sales smarts allow you to sit down. If any customers are passing by, be on your feet to speak the inviting comments or just to say, "How are you today?" Remember, don't say, "May I help you?" Stand up and walk over to greet any customer. I find it is fatal to sales if we sit on our backsides and stare at them if they are stopping to look.

Don't Complain!

Don't complain about anything. Don't say, "I'm so tired I could drop," or "I'm glad this is the last day. I'm about dead," or "I wish six o'clock would come soon," or "I wonder why the promoters didn't advertise this show better. There are no customers here." Complaining and griping have no place in any business setting. Leave your personal problems at home and smile no matter how you feel. Don't tell anyone how stressful the show has been.

Don't Talk with Your Other Salespeople

Don't talk with other salespeople in the booth about anything other than how to make this show better. Don't discuss your children, your family, your grandchildren, your husband, or your health with the other employees in the booth. You have not been paid to stand in the booth and visit as a social time. If you talk about your children, your grandchildren, or your family, do it with the customers. Sometimes they like to tell you about their families, and you might share a little bit about yours if it is appropriate. A good way to open this type of conversation is, "Tell me about your family." Most everyone loves to talk about her/his family, especially women.

Thank Everybody

Thank everybody for their business and comment on what good choices they have made. Tell them that you believe they will enjoy their products and tell them where your name and address are in the materials they have just obtained in case they have further questions about the product. Your best customers probably should be given your home phone also. I have almost never had a customer call me at home; however, it is a great way to let your customers know how much you value them.

Gaining the Maximum Profit from Trade Shows

Have Bags for Each Customer

Sometimes sellers seem to forget that they will be selling a product that needs a bag in which to send it home. This is poor business. We always have extra bags in case someone else has not provided a bag. We offer to give them another bag in which to put all of their purchases. We prefer plastic bags with handles with which customers can easily get back to their car. Hopefully they will reuse the bag over and over if it is a decent bag. Many people go to the expense of putting their name and phone numbers on a bag so people will have the means by which to communicate with the dealer if they would like more of the product.

Many times we do not use printed bags because they are expensive. The few times we have run out of our clear plastic bags, we have stopped at a grocery store in the morning and purchased plastic bags. Please always have a bag to give.

Use Giveaways

If possible, try to have something to give away. This can be as simple as one sheet of instructions, such as "Simple tricks for displaying antiques in different rooms," or "Easy ways to get better pictures of your children and grandchildren," or "Displaying your dolls and teddy bears." You might write a little paper about "Using crafts to decorate your family room or kitchen," or "History of the Ford automobile," or "How electronics have changed." Then you can say to everybody who comes by your booth, "Would you like a free handout on _____?" In our booths, we give a free *Sew Beautiful* magazine. Of course, we believe that when people get home and look at this magazine loaded with free patterns, color pictures, beautiful designs, and professional editorials, they are going to want to subscribe. Having something free means that you can reach out and invite everyone to look at your products in a nice way.

Create a Mailing List from Attendees

Get a mailing list of people who would like to be sent a catalog or other mailings. Type them into the computer as soon as you get home and categorize it as "_____ Craft Show, March 23, 1998." Sometimes I send a letter to each person on my mailing list thanking them for coming by and telling them when the next catalog will be sent. This is an outrageously nice service and very unexpected. Now isn't that the best type of customer service?

Don't Repeat Staff Miscasting

If your relatives can't sell and can't follow all of the above rules, leave them at home! Hire someone who can help your business or just go by yourself. Another difficult booth staffing decision is when you have taken an employee several times to a show and you realize that this individual really isn't a good salesperson/people person after all. It is best to not invite that employee to travel to the next show. Sometimes this can be difficult if this is a valuable employee in some other area of the business but he/she simply doesn't have the people skills for selling.

"It Was a GREAT Show!"

At the end of the show, tell everyone that it was a great show. Nothing beats any industry down like gripers and complainers who tell the whole world that they didn't get rich during this show. Instead you might have gained new names for your mailing list, new customers who will buy from you later on. I have never been to a show where I did not gain valuable contacts! Every person I had the opportunity to meet *is a valuable contact*!

Seminars at Shows

. Trade shows offer seminars to attendees as a method to increase the value of the show to them and as a way to give more exposure to those with booths. I am able to speak to sometimes 250 attendees at one time when I give a seminar at a trade show. Many of these individuals walk right out of the presentation and into my booth and buy. If I had to present hour-long information individually in the booth, it wouldn't be possible.

Start Associations and Users Groups

One of the best ways to promote your business is to create associations and users groups for those who use your product or service. Even if there is already a national group, consider creating a local group. Associations and users groups meet to work on similar issues, concerns, and interests. Providing an excellent outlet in which they can meet and learn not only serves them and your industry, but it also brings a huge number of your customers all together at the same time. As the "sponsor" of the event, you gain incredible exposure. You make additional income from creating a "trade show" at these events and selling space to other vendors.

Kenneth V. F. Blanchard is an African-American whose hobby is guns. He started a gun club, called the Tenth Cavalry Gun Club, named after the U.S. Army regiments also known as the "Buffalo Soldiers." Through the club he gets advertisement, help, marketing information, and future customers. "When I successfully grow the club in all the states, I will change the face of the shooting sports, leading the way." He sells logo items from the gun club, gun safety courses, memberships to the club, and monologues.

Forums and Newsgroups as Marketing Tools

Newsgroups and forums are cyber-services. They are an excellent source of information and networking. They allow you to take part in communities of people interested in particular topics. They offer the unique opportunity to participate in discussions on a wide range of subjects.

You are able to post questions and watch a "thread" develop as people give their input to that question. These threads are smaller conversations within the larger topic of the newsgroups or forums. For example, a group about pets may contain threads about dogs, cats, iguanas, and other animals.

When you get to an area you think you are interested in, look for FAQ (Frequently Asked Questions) documents. These documents point you in the right direction. They also generally discuss etiquette for Internet participative areas. "Netiquette" is the recommended conduct for individuals who use the Internet. We suggest before you plunge into these areas, you "lurk." Lurking means you read through the posts before offering your own contribution. Lurking helps you find out what has already been said and how the newsgroup works.

You can also create your own newsgroups or forums as a service to your customers. Go to your on-line service or your search engine on your Internet server and do a search using "create newsgroups." You find many articles that will explain how it is done within your own computer and Internet set up.

Go to your on-line search engine for your on-line services and on the Internet and search using "forum" for lists of what is available. Look for groups that discuss your topic. It is a great way to network and learn.

Usenet Newsgroups (also referred to as Usenet, newsgroups, or just News) connect millions of people around the world. These newsgroups are distributed through the Internet—you'll find more than twenty thousand topics in these globe-spanning discussions. You can access newsgroups from your on-line service or directly from the Internet. Go to your on-line search engine for your on-line services and/or on the Internet and search using "newsgroup" for lists of what is available.

Listen and Observe Your Customers: A Wholesale Business Is Born

A vital step in promoting your business is to listen and observe what your customers say they want.

Ours is a very small targeted industry—French laces and Swiss goods were simply not available in the vast majority of towns in the United States. For a long time we were successful in selling products through trade shows several times a year. But small shop owners tell me that travel to a trade show is costly and takes too much time away from their business. They would rather take that expense money and purchase inventory. It makes sense since nearly all of the credible wholesalers have good catalogs. People started calling our retail store trying to imagine colors of fabrics and patterns of laces over the phone. Many requests came in for a catalog so they could purchase goods for smocking and French sewing. I listened and observed—we started a catalog.

Bill Marriott had a restaurant in Washington, D.C. One day, a waitress complained about "those darn travelers," always wanting her to make up meals to bring on the planes. "Such a big bother." Marriott listened and observed. Ever wonder who makes most of those meals on planes now? Look out your plane window at those trucks bringing in the food, all owned by Marriott! Those little Host restaurants in most airports? Yupp! Marriott again.

—Dottie and Lilly Walters,
*101 Simple Things to Grow
Your Business and Yourself!*

Creating a Catalog

We started with a homemade catalog. When I say homemade, I mean photocopied sheets. Guess what? It worked wonderfully. Our next inexpensive catalog was done at a rural newspaper office and run off like a newspaper. It worked great also.

We felt the need to create a more sophisticated catalog, so we had a couple of color catalogs made but they were expensive. We used the "catalog color printers" because they gave the best prices; however, it was still expensive and a lot of trouble to photograph things in color, get separations made, etc. We decided to go to a larger catalog and still have photocopied sheets of the exact sizes of laces, embroideries, and other items. We went to another newspaper location and discovered that they could do a little booklet with very high grade newsprint. Since we need a fifty-four-page catalog, this is simply the most economical way to get one.

One day we will do a complete color catalog. With fifty-four pages this is quite an undertaking, both in people resources and printing cost. I am reminded of the old saying, "If it isn't broken, don't fix it." That really applies to our catalog situation since the newsprint catalog has worked quite well for us for seventeen years.

Becoming a Legend in Catalog Sales

We became a legend in the sewing catalog business by using these strategies:

- Ever-growing mailing lists: Gather names and addresses everywhere you go.
- Bulk mail: We use a great bulk mail house.
- Piggyback mailings: We send our catalogs in a plastic bag along with the *Sew Beautiful* magazines. It is cheaper that way.
- Personalization: Our whole business is a personal business. I love to write personal notes beside items in the catalog telling why I love it or why it is a great bargain.

People magazine is one of the best selling in the world. People love news about other people. Please make your catalog personal. Look at L.L. Bean who uses real people who work in different departments to model the clothing. I write a personal letter in the beginning of each catalog telling what's new and what we are up to at Martha Pullen Company. Our customers know my children and grandchildren by name because I tell our important family news in the catalog. I always loved hearing about Wal-Mart's Sam Walton and his family and about how he still drove an old red truck and lived in an ordinary house. I loved knowing anything personal about him and especially how he remained a real person while being one of the richest men in the world.

I use that philosophy of making things personal in my catalog. I love to give bargains; however, you have to tell your customers that they are bargains. I love to send discount coupons. I date my coupons and the customers must mail them in; that saves us the cost of a 1-800 phone call, therefore we can give good discounts. We try always to have something new in the catalog. Having good products, great prices, personal news and touches, and sales that are dated are great things to use in a catalog.

Let me state once more that those photocopied sheets served us well for many years. People need to know what you have and homemade is a great start. If you have a computer and know how to scan things in and do decent layout, then spend some time and do it. For a brand new catalog for a person without those skills and little money, then photocopy away. It worked for us.

How I Got My Television Show

As we grew we realized we would reach more people—without my traveling every day of the year—if we could do a television series. We quickly found out that we couldn't afford to pay a private studio to film twenty-six shows. My mama always taught me, "There is more than one way to skin a rabbit."

I called the Alabama Center for Public Television in Tuscaloosa and they were interested in becoming my partner in this venture. We decided that underwriters could pay the small amount of initial filming time and that they would be my partners in the selling of the videos. In short, they make the profit off the video sales and I make the profit from the book sales. This has been a financially sound venture for us both. If they hadn't believed in me and my idea, we probably wouldn't have a television show today.

A satisfied customer is the world's greatest advertising agent. Our customers simply set up a national network in their own corners of their worlds and proceeded to get "Martha's Sewing Room" on the air. Within eight months, "Martha's Sewing Room" was airing somewhere in forty-four of the fifty U.S. states. What joy to our hearts that a Southern woman teaching heirloom sewing would be well received in every part of the United States. At this time it has now aired in all fifty states.

National Underwriters

A national underwriter for PBS television programming is someone who will pay a certain amount of money to cover the cost of the production. We were fortunate to have several who were willing to pay this amount. The advantage to you of getting a national underwriter is financial, obviously, but also it is to have the prestige of important companies thinking your project is worthy.

Getting Your Own Cable Television Show

Having a television show on a big network is a wonderful dream. But it is a dream that will take a great deal of work. However, local cable television has public access that they must supply to the community and are looking for a neat little show, maybe one you would produce about your hobby!

Just pick up your phone book, and note the local cable television companies in your area. Call and ask for the company manager or public access manager. Simply ask them how you go about getting airtime. Often these companies even provide production support if you have a good idea. You do all the writing of the show, get the guests, come up with themes. That's the good news. The bad news is they don't have a large audience. But you will have tape that you can use to promote your idea to bigger stations. If the show is a good one, the cable station will even promote it to other cable stations. Your program might be shown all over the USA! You don't do this for money; you do it for exposure.

How to Get in the News

Obtaining free publicity in the media is an effective way to attract customers and build your image as a legend! There is one little problem with getting the media to promote you: They have no interest in promoting you. But if you help the media with what they are interested in, publicity for you and your business will follow. What does the media want? The media wants their circulation and/or ratings to increase to enable them to profit from their advertisers. To do that, they want to deliver fascinating, exciting, helpful material to their readers or audiences.

You can meet their needs by finding ways to be newsworthy, searching for the "hooks," taking surveys, getting a "you" attitude, and targeting the right media.

Find Ways to Be Newsworthy

To have the press eager to work for you, find things about your hobby that are "newsworthy." Look for stories involving

- ways someone's life has been changed by the hobby
- anyone famous that also does the same hobby
- ancient history about your hobby
- unusual people among your students or clients: e.g., someone very young, very old, handicapped
- ways your hobby is related to whatever is going on in the press at the moment
- when you or anyone associated with your hobby or company
    - holds an event
    - receives an honor

- is elected to an office
- has a book published
- a good photo opportunity while doing your hobby. Encourage someone with a camera to keep it loaded and ready. Have black and white photos of you professionally done, preferably in an action shot.

If you are still at a loss for a "hook," look at your newspaper. You will often become inspired with "hooks" or PR "gimmicks" just by seeing the sorts of things currently in print.

Years ago, I was teaching in New Zealand and the local paper wanted to do a story on me. The photographer surrounded me with children who were dressed for the fashion show. We all got our heads close together, and there I was encircled by these gorgeous children's faces. This was quite a picture and I have since had that picture duplicated for black and white publicity photographs back in Huntsville. I also had another publicity shot done with me at a tea party with children and my daughter, Joanna, dressed in Victorian clothing.

Newspapers and television stations love using real people, not just business people. Have people told you that your teaching or store or hobby has helped them get through a very difficult time in their lives? Has a grandmother made twenty-two dolls for all of her family for Christmas? Has a customer gone to the senior citizens center to teach a skill learned from you? Has someone made Christmas gifts for residents of a nursing home to give to their families? You or one of your customers being involved in volunteer work for those less fortunate is almost always a newsworthy idea. Our best *free* publicity ideas often center on people helping other people.

You have to call the newspaper or write up a story and put it in a reporter's hands. Sometimes there isn't a need for the story at that particular time; but reporters have to dig up stories just like the rest of us have to create ideas. It never hurts to let your television stations, newspapers, and radio stations know about creative things happening in your business. For most of us, we have to be our own public relations agent because we can't afford to hire one. It can be done.

Get a Hook, Get a Gimmick, Be Unusual

Have I mentioned I have not always been brilliant in the steps I have taken? Some of the best PR I ever got was, well . . .

Things were exciting during the fall of 1962. I had been chosen as a University of Alabama cheerleader, and Joe Namath was our star. On January 1, 1963, we were in the Orange Bowl, and President John F. Kennedy attended the game! Oh my, I idolized President Kennedy with all the adoration of a nineteen-year-old. I wanted to see the President more than anything else in the world; so at half-time, I gathered up my crimson and white pom poms and headed around the field to get a real look at my idol. There he was: my President. I did just what you would imagine any happy young cheerleader would do fulfilling her life's dream . . . I wept. No, I sobbed. He looked down and saw me sobbing and sent a secret service man down to invite me up to his box. As he introduced himself and everyone else in the box, I continued to sob my eyes out. Finally he said to me, "Your team is doing very well today." I nodded, and with great eloquence, cried some more.

Impressed with my facility with words, our President smiled and said, "What is your name?" Getting a grip, I took a deep breath, and cried harder. My name? I had no idea. Finally I mumbled through my tears, "Mr. President, thank you so much for allowing me to come to meet you." Then I sobbed some more. At which point I gave it up, turned, and walked down the stairs accompanied by a Miami police officer who was no doubt ready to give me a blood test.

Had I known anything about PR at the time, I would have been more appreciative of the moment. The Orange Bowl Queen was waving in the middle of the half-time show, but all cameras were on me. When I arrived at the bottom of the stairs, every photographer and camera man at the Orange Bowl was waiting for me.

The next day, who gets half a page in the *Miami Herald* doing a spread eagle cheerleading jump? You guessed it, me. Who gets one-eighth-page on the back page? The Orange Bowl Queen. Who got one-fourth-page on the same page with me? President John F. Kennedy.

The Associated Press had sent my picture with the title "Speech Major Forgets Her Name When Meeting Kennedy" to every paper in the U.S. and my picture appeared on the front page of most U.S. papers. Overnight I became famous! What a pity I stumbled onto a great hook way back then when I didn't need it. Today I am a publicity hound, constantly on the hunt for ways to promote my business. We need to search for unusual things if we want free publicity. The press is always looking for unusual stories, and it is up to us to find those stories within our daily routine and create an unusual hook for the press to bite.

Kenneth V. F. Blanchard capitalized on being unique to turn his hobby to profit. As mentioned earlier, he is an African-American whose hobby is guns. He turned his passion to profit by becoming one of the most recognized experts on the subject of guns and African-American issues. "My law enforcement background, positive image, and speaking energy has made me a nice novelty in the firearms community. There are many people of color that participate in the shooting sports. I am unique because of my law enforcement background, and my viewpoint is often contrary to the opinion spoken aloud in my community. I use my uniqueness to help others locate me, hence the business name African American Arms & Instruction, Inc. Though it is a mouthful, it helps others in identifying that there are other ethnicities in the shooting sports despite popular opinion to the contrary."

When in Doubt, Take a Survey

One simple and effective hook is to take a survey. Take a good long look at the people buying things related to your hobby. Ask them, for example, what three things they wished they had related to your hobby. When you compile the results, you may find some interesting ideas for ways to profit from your hobby. Also, by assessing their needs, and researching solutions, you will become known as the subject "expert," someone who gets paid for their expertise.

Often the material you develop in your survey can become additional income-producing products: reports, newsletters, books, audio tapes, video albums, or CDs. There is nothing like talking to the people who are out in the business world to find out what is really going on.

Get a "You" Attitude

Attract the media's attention by getting the "you" attitude into your public relations, promotion, and advertising ("How You Can Overcome . . ." "New Method to Obtain . . .").

Study the titles of successful products. Good titles state the benefit clearly: "Wheaties! The Breakfast of Champions!" or "Frosted Flakes, They're Great!"—both immediately stating or implying benefits to the customer of either good health or good taste. Test every word of copy you write to promote your business against this yardstick: "Is there a benefit for the buyer in every word?"

When you are knowledgeable in your subject and present it in a helpful and interesting style to the appropriate media, you will find your stories appearing in print and on the air.

Target the Right Media

Once you think of "hooks" for your business and write up your PR with a "you" attitude, you need to find media people who "care" about what you do.

Target the Right Writer

Look through the newspaper and note the "bylines." Bylines are the credit lines given to the author of articles. This is the person who found the subject, conducted the interview, and wrote the article. Watch for bylines on articles that are the same type of story you would like to see written about you and your business.

Call the publication and ask for the writer of a specific story. By asking for the writer by name, you go right to the person who may want to write a story about your type of business. Tip: Always let the writer know how much you enjoyed their other article, then let them know your story idea.

Target the Right Publications

If your topic is boating, you should not call the beauty editor of a magazine or newspaper, or the host of a beauty show on television or radio, unless you can slant your topic effectively to their subject. For example, if you have a bed and breakfast by the ocean, and you want to get some press in health or beauty media, you could offer articles or interviews on "How Fresh Salt Air Cures Skin Ailments."

To Find the Appropriate Media Contacts

All the newspapers, radio stations, and television stations in your area are listed in your phone book. To find national media contacts, try the Web or the reference librarian at your local library. In addition to the obvious large publications, major magazines, and newspapers, you might find a greater value in these:

- Company publications: If you can think of the right hook for your articles, you will often get company publications, who are hungry for interesting articles about what is going on in their own community, to publish them.
- Trade journals: Ask your customers which trade journals they read. Make it a point to locate and contact those publications with an article! It is often much easier to get started writing for trade journals than for major publications. When you write for a specific company publication

or association newsletter, put the name of their group in your headline. For example, the topic "How CPAs Can _____" would be ideal for an accounting publication.

- Small publications and newsletters: these media frequently will be delighted to print your articles, if your material offers benefits to their readers and is the right length and style.

- Become a columnist: Your column can appear in anything from the local weekly to trade publications in your field. Often these publications will run your address and phone number at the end of the article or column, especially if you offer a free piece of information, a list, or other important and helpful information to those who contact you.

Create a Press Database

Call each company and find the correct contact(s) who might be interested in your area of expertise. Always create a database of these names. Add them to your master promotional mailing list. Make sure all the smaller, local media know about you. These smaller radio, TV, and newspaper contacts are the ones most eager to do stories about you. Call them personally about upcoming events, and fax, mail, and E-mail them press releases.

Never Give Up

I have attempted to share with you lots of ways I have wiggled my way into getting publicity over the years. Creativity is the key if you can't afford a public relations person or agency. As in all sales, pick up the phone and tell people what you would like to see happen. Invite the media to come to see what you are doing. Be excited and get them excited. Send balloons after your conversation to thank them for your time on the phone. Get their E-mail addresses and send thanks to them. There is something about a personal E-mail that almost makes one a friend with the other person. Sending even a

Godiva chocolate candy bar is special and only costs a few dollars.

Always send a personal thank-you note after anybody tries to help you in any way. You don't have to write a whole note, just write in big letters THANK YOU SO VERY MUCH FOR YOUR KINDNESS! and sign your name. I sign all of my letters, "May God Bless You, Martha." If that isn't comfortable for you, a "Sincerely yours" will do nicely also. Don't ever give up, don't ever give up, don't ever give up on trying to get free publicity and advertising.

God has opened all of my doors for me. He has the best contacts of all, and he can open all doors if they are the right ones and in his plan for you.

Ask and it will be given to you; seek and you will find; knock and the door will be opened to you. For everyone who asks receives; he who seeks finds; and to him who knocks, the door will be opened.
—Matthew 7:7–8

CHAPTER ELEVEN

Using Publications, Classes, and Events

Promotional Publications: Newsletters and Magazines

Creating your own books, newsletters, and magazines is a great source of income and of promotions. We found that creating our own publications was a brilliant source of PR. They act as promotional soldiers, marching out into the world and sending business back to you when you least expect it. Someone buys one of our books or magazines and gives it to a friend, who gives it to another friend. Years later we get a call from someone asking, "Do you still offer your seminars?" It is amazing how publications keep working for you for years.

Lives Are Touched Farther Away Than You Know

A well-created work will keep acting to enhance the lives of those who read it. Neal Petersen was born with only one complete hip joint. "The books I read as a child made a huge impact on my life. It was the knowledge from books that inspired me to live my dreams." As a handicapped, "colored" child in apartheid-torn South Africa, he had few friends to play with. Neal found himself drawn to hobbies: reading books and magazines about the sea. To strengthen his legs after many operations, prior to being allowed to put any weight on his legs, he was taught to swim. He was able to find ways to make his new hobby pay even as a child, "When other boys could kick a ball, I could hunt lobsters!" says Petersen. "I scrubbed hulls of yachts in a local marina. I spent what I earned on buying books. In the years after, my saved earnings resulted in my designing and building a 38-foot racing yacht, another hobby!" He became a unique and champion caliber yatchsman. Things have gone full circle: "My own book, an autobiography, *No Barriers*, was published (Brookside, Dublin). Currently my book is being made into a motion picture. I am involved in product promotions, sports endorsements, sponsorships, and public relations, all as a result of living what is still my hobbies."

Traditional Publishing vs. Self-Publishing

If you produce your own publications, you will be a self-publisher. If someone else does it, we can call it a traditional publisher. Both have advantages.

Having Someone Else Publish Your Products

There are all kinds of publishers, big and small, that might want to publish your product for you. On the downside, you have no control over production—they might create something that is simply awful, edit it past what you recognize, and you have no say-so. The normal publisher will print two thousand of your books, put it in their standard catalog, and wait to see what happens. The majority of books published go no farther than that first run of two thousand.

On the upside, with a publisher you receive an advance deposit against royalties. The publisher will deal with all production issues and costs: typesetting, editing, printing problems, ISBN, bar coding, and cover design. They market the book into bookstores and often to book clubs.

Being published will help you turn your hobby to profit in many ways, so do not give up. The odds against your product being published by a major publisher are high, especially on a first product. Publishers receive thousands of unsolicited manuscripts per year. It is estimated that 350,000 books are actually written annually, but not submitted to publishers. Only 32,000 books actually go into print each year in the United States. Do not be hurt by rejection letters. If getting published were easy, everyone would do it.

Ann Ball's hobbies were writing and "saint collecting." She states, "I was teaching and began collecting photos of the modern saints to show my students that these were real people, not just plaster statues. One day I realized that I had information on over 100 of these people and that I needed to share the information with more people than just my own students."

Ann told us her greatest challenge was finding a publisher for that first book. She developed the motto: "If at first you don't succeed, try, try again!" Ann's perseverance and love of her hobbies has today led her to a second career in writing. You can see some of her work in the Barnes and Noble Internet site, and she is a regular contributor to several national Catholic publications. "After my first book was published, I began to write more . . . both books and articles. During the day I run a security guard company; at night I creep home and write religious stuff. Guns to nuns, bad guys to saints."

Self-Publishing

I sold over a quarter of a million of my sewing books by self-publishing. If we had gone with a traditional publisher, we would have received 10 to

When I first tried to find a publisher, I think that every major Catholic publisher turned me down. I used to joke that I was going to wallpaper the bathroom with them. After the first tears of the first reject, I began to read what the rejects said. Most were form letters simply saying 'it's not for us' but some were real letters saying that at the time (late 70s) religious publishing was in trouble because people just weren't buying 'religious' books and that the photos would make the project extra expensive and thus a big gamble. No one said my idea or my writing was bad. Finally, after many rejections, I located a publisher who was willing to gamble on the idea. I firmly believe that God gives each of us talents but expects us, like the servants of the parables, to try hard to use what he has given us.[6]

15 percent per book, about one dollar for a small book. When we self-published, we made a much higher profit per book. When you self-publish, you can expect 75 percent and more markup on your production costs. You receive all the income from sales because you personally did all the work a major publisher usually does. You are the perfect person to produce your books and products; you are already committed to their success! Besides, no one knows your market like you. A publisher may take two years to produce a book, you can do it in months.

Producing product yourself is relatively inexpensive. Audio tapes can be produced for seventy-five cents to three dollars each. Some books can be printed for two to four dollars each if you print ten thousand. Of course thick, hardcover books are more expensive.

If your self-published product sells well, you will have proven that there is a market. Successful self-publishing can set you up as a good prospect for a book contract from a major publisher.

Newsletters

One of the best and most economical ways to become known quickly and to promote your product or service is to publish your own newsletter. Newsletters get passed along to friends and associates in many organizations.

Begin with an annual or bi-annual newsletter. Then expand it to quarterly or bi-monthly if you feel it is appropriate. Someday it might become so valuable that you charge for subscriptions. Write interesting, quick, and easy-to-read tips, ideas, and information that you know people are hungry for. The sort of newsletters that are read, and act as valuable advertising pieces, are those that have great value to your customers. If it is just a puff piece for yourself, it will get tossed. If it just says, "Come buy stuff from me, I'm great," it will get tossed. With a value-laden newsletter, your customers will soon begin to associate you and your company as *the* person to contact whenever they think about your special area.

You can mail your newsletter (which might be one legal-size sheet printed on both sides) to past, present, and future buyers, or consider sending it via fax or E-mail. Set it up on your computer so that it goes out automatically. With today's technology, you can produce a simple newsletter from the templates provided in almost all word processing software. They even have spelling and grammar checks for you. Electronic newsletters (newsletters sent out via E-mail) are almost free to send, immediate, and so easy a child can do it.

How to Start a Magazine

A magazine is a much bigger investment than a newsletter, but it is obviously a bigger income-producing and prestige item. A magazine can often grow out of your newsletter.

To create your own successful magazine, you need to:

- Identify a need.
- Learn to do the layout and graphics or hire a layout person. If you were able to learn this for your newsletter, you might be able to produce a simple magazine. Chances are you will need to hire a professional.
- Have an automatic audience at the beginning. Have the market and the mailing list ready to go.
- Be prepared to write most of it yourself. I wrote nearly all of the magazine for the first few years.
- Have lots of good friends who will contribute articles.
- Deliver quality. Produce a gorgeous product so companies will want to advertise.
- Make it personal.

Selling Via Education: Giving Classes and Major Events

One filled with joy preaches without preaching.
—Mother Teresa (1910–1997),
Albanian Roman Catholic missionary

Becoming a "speaker" or "teacher" is a magnificent way to promote any business. When you speak at a meeting, dinner, or conference, to a class in your shop, or to a room full of potential buyers in your community, you will be addressing a room full of prospects. Can you create a talk that is fun and informative? If so, you can promote your business beyond your wildest dreams, with no investment of money—just the investment of your ideas, hopes, and helpfulness.

Teach 'Em and Sell 'Em

I never had many customers run though the doors and say, "Martha, I absolutely must have this brand of sewing machine! Wrap it up! By the way, what's the price?" Rather, I found it necessary to use a bit of creativity to make the machine sales. I decided to show my potential customers how wonderful my machine was and why it would be beneficial to their lives.

My formula for selling sewing machines was to get the machines into the classroom and teach new techniques. There is nothing as effective in sales as having the customer take possession of a product. Once they touch it, feel it, and use it, it becomes part of them. Car dealers or horse traders have been using the "test drive" method for years! By using education to attract them, the customer is able to experience the benefits of your product or service.

Do not ever sell anything or talk about selling anything while the class is in session. It makes the class participants mad and they probably won't buy anything from you anyway! If the class is great, people will want more of the product and your service—not from advertising, not from gimmicks, but from education.

Speak to a Room Full of Prospects

I cannot think of a better way to use your teaching skills to promote and sell your business locally than to get out and speak to every local service and civic organization imaginable. Do you realize what you would pay for advertising to fifty prominent customers, such as those who attend civic clubs? Can you imagine getting twenty minutes of people's time in their office to tell your story? Well, you can do just that by teaching in the form of a good informational program to civic clubs and even free in "public seminars."

Create an interesting twenty-minute program relating to your business and get started. The program needs to be educational rather than "Buy my product/service." Don't sell directly but rather inform generally about a topic of interest to nearly everyone. At the end, you can give out business cards and a brochure to those interested in learning more about your topic.

I called the Chamber of Commerce in Huntsville and asked for the names and addresses of all the civic clubs. After assuring them of my intentions, the list was sent. There were more than 250 civic clubs and organizations that have weekly or monthly meetings in Huntsville/Madison County, and we only have 175,000 people! Some clubs meet fifty-two weeks of the year and need programs for each of those meetings.

Using Tabletop Clinics to Get New Customers in the Door

Tabletop clinics are basically demonstrations that take place on the top of a table. Simple enough? We have used tabletop clinics in my schools for years. It is "sort of" the same thing as demonstrating in a booth at a craft show. Teaching with whatever you can put on a table is the whole idea. What are some of the advantages of a tabletop clinic?

- fun way to let customers know you care about them—great rapport builder
- good way to get people into the door to see the whole atmosphere of your business and obtain new prospects
- great way to get an expanded mailing list
- exceptionally great way to show your new products

- great sales technique through educational means
- you can plan each individualized presentation around customer's needs
- greatest way to sell "without selling"

These clinics can provide opportunities for future contacts:

- Write a thank-you note to all who came for the free tabletop clinic.
- When a customer is interested in a product, make an appointment to share more with him/her at another date. Remind them of the appointment date when you send a thank-you note.
- Some people indicate that about two or three qualified appointments can be made if twenty people are contacted. If you have 100 people in the door for the tabletop clinics, attempt to make at least ten appointments for more in-depth appointments to show the product more thoroughly.

Producing the "Big Event"

We have been extremely successful by creating a celebrity event, The Martha Pullen School of Art Fashion. We have about 220–300 people at one of these four-day events. You can apply this "big event" concept to your business whether your business is a bicycle shop, a bakery, a construction company, a real estate agency, a physician's office, a dress shop, or any other type of business. Once again, this big event is a hands-on, educational experience. The formula is

- create an event, with a celebrity to pull in attendance
- get the best teachers, preferably authors
- have lesson plans required by all teachers
- get the schedule ready
- be well organized
- make it personal

Details for a Big Event

Usually we do events on Thursday, Friday, Saturday, and Sunday. As an added personal touch, we have a Sunday school early on Sunday morning for all those who would like to attend.

The following "how-to" information for a four-day big event can be used for any number of people, and you divide the people into four sections.

Teachers/Celebrities

- Getting four celebrity teachers is fairly easy and not too expensive. "Celebrity" in many industries means someone who has written a book or been published in magazines or done a video.
- You might use two celebrity teachers and two excellent local teachers. However, hiring celebrity teachers usually is better than hiring local teachers.
- Have a teacher contract drawn up so both of you can sign it.
- Cover things such as teaching fee per day, meal per diem allowed and how it will be paid, transportation to and from the airport, who will pick up your teacher and return him/her to the airport, and having the teacher give the hotel a personal credit card upon arrival so the teacher can cover all personal phone calls, meals not covered under your arrangement, and other things which you will not be paying for.

Hotel or Convention Facility

- Get a hotel or facility that will handle your classes as well as your lunch and dinner meals, if you choose to include dinner in your groups.
- Usually a hotel will give you free teaching rooms if you have at least one meal a day in the facility. Bargain and look around for hotels or conference centers.
- Negotiate with your hotel for free teaching rooms for a certain number of student rooms rented.

- Check on security for your rooms from the hotel. We leave sewing machines in the rooms, so we can't be lax about security.
- Know who will have the teaching room keys at all times.
- We prefer to use average-priced hotels.

Electricity and Audio Visual Equipment

- You must know the electricity requirements that your teachers and students will need. Check with the hotel electricians to be sure the electricity is adequate. We do sewing seminars, so we need electrical outlets for each person to have a sewing machine as well as a light.
- Work with the audio equipment people to have things such as microphones, overhead projectors, screens, shades on the windows for correct lighting, and slide projectors as needed. These things must be in proper working order. Two times I have arrived on Saturday morning for a major fashion show and slide show, and the light bulb was burned out on the projector.

Pre-Event Promotion

- You have to let your prospective students know well in advance about the event.
- I think planning a big event at least a year in advance is advantageous. This gives people a chance to plan their schedules and to plan for the cost of the event.
- Advertise in your usual places: radio, newspaper, bulletin boards, etc.
- Get brochures ready to mail.
- Your newsletter is one of the best places to inform people of the exciting event that is coming up.
- *Get a deposit of at least one-fourth on the event admission to hold someone a place.* Be specific about refunding a deposit and when you will refund the deposit. Have a computer program of some type for entering the people and their deposit.

- Send out reminders and happy news about the event to inform them what supplies to bring, about the discounts you will offer while they are there, and anything else you would like to tell them. This keeps them excited and wanting to tell their friends about the event.

Insurance

- Check with your business insurance to see if it covers events like this in a hotel for personal injury and other possible events.
- Check with your hotel or facility about their insurance coverage in the event of an accident. We have had people fall down in the hotel, and one student's child crawled under the dresser and ate some bug poison. Thank God both were rushed to the hospital and everything was all right. However, you and your hotel should have some written understandings about their hotel coverage of your guests.
- I do not allow any of my employees to drive students anywhere in Huntsville in their personal vehicles. My company van and my company car are the only private vehicles that I knowingly allow my students to ride in. They are insured for Martha Pullen Company business events.
- We state on the brochure that all liability for students' personal equipment they bring is their liability. Neither Martha Pullen Company nor the hotel is responsible for any loss of their personal equipment. We tell our students to cover their sewing machines on their homeowner's insurance before they bring it.

Classes

- We run our classes from nine to twelve and from three to five.
- We have scheduled breaks in the morning and afternoon with snacks and drinks. This is not necessary but we always do it.

- The teachers need good lesson plans if these classes are hands-on.
- Kits need to be ready and neat.
- Tables need to be adequate for the projects if the projects are hands-on.
- All equipment needs to be either in the kit or available to buy in the store.
- We send supply lists to the students several weeks before the classes. This is not necessary if you are going to supply everything in the kits or if the classes are not to be hands-on.

Retail Store in the Hotel

- You need to sell things during "off hours" while the students are with you for the event.
- We use a teaching room in the hotel or a suite with the furniture moved out to set up a retail store.
- Always give the largest discounts that you can possibly afford to give when the students are there. Have your teachers give you a large discount on their books, patterns, etc., as well.

Lunch Activities

- We give door prizes at lunch.
- Getting everyone's name into a bag is easy. Either run them off from your computer student list or get everyone to sign in the first day on a little slip.
- Draw from the same bag each day so one person won't get more than one door prize.
- If there is to be a grand prize on the last day, get another bag with everyone's name in the bag.

Dinner at Our Home

- We invite all students to our home for a catered barbecue at our house one evening.
- We give maps for students who have their own cars.

- We hire a bus for those students who do not have transportation.
- Sometimes the students offer rides to other students. *We do not suggest it for insurance reasons. We furnish an insured ride for everyone.*
- Have all food served purchased from a licensed catering service. The insurance liability is too great to serve any homemade food. Besides, it is against the health department laws to serve homemade food to business guests. Don't take this risk. Hotels won't allow any food to be brought into the hotel unless it comes from a licensed catering service or bakery or grocery store. Usually they won't allow any food to be brought in from anywhere; you must serve their food for meals as well as snacks for breaks.

Other Evening Event Possibilities

- A tabletop clinic is a fun night where teachers, as well as other business people, present a tabletop demonstration of many different types. We usually have a potato/salad buffet bar for the evening meal.
- I use a combination slide and fashion show for my evening large group presentations. Fashion shows can be done with things other than clothing. People can walk with the latest in equipment and simply have a microphone narration about the new product. We have had sewing machine fashion shows where the machine was carried while the commentary was going on about the new product. These are fun and very unusual.
- Students love to participate in evening "show and tells," whether it is in "modeling" or in a "drag and brag" time.

Banquet Saturday Night

- Banquets are fun and festive even if you don't have entertainment such as a fashion show.
- Don't plan on a band and dancing if you just have women or men in attendance. Besides, bands are expensive.

Testing and Enhancing New Marketing and Business Ideas

As you can see from all of the ideas on promotion I have discussed so far, there are many different directions you can take. It can be overwhelming as to which ones to take. Often we have someone on our team come up with "a great new idea." We have learned to sit down as a team to do some serious brainstorming to nurture or get rid of the idea. Here is what we do:

- Decide what you want to sell.
- Brainstorm every possible good idea and bad idea about that dream. *Write them down!*
- (This particular activity is for me alone. I would never ask my employees to spend eight hours on one project at one time.) Spend eight hours, by the clock, writing down every thought about selling that product that comes to your mind. Pay no attention to organization, reality, or nonreality; just write down every thought and question that comes to mind about your desire to sell that product. Some possible questions to answer are:

  - What is the least creative business that I can think of which sells this product?
  - What is the most creative business that I can think of which sells this product?
  - How can I find new people to whom I can sell this product?
  - How can I make these people want to buy this product from me rather than from someone else?
  - Do I need a catalog?
  - Do I need salespeople on the road?
  - What kind of advertising do I need?

Becoming a Legend with GRACE

As you create promotional strategies that bring the customers in to look at your "mouse trap," go forward with

GRACE. Don't be a brilliant artist sitting at home painting with no sales!

We work daily at becoming a legend through the methods we have talked about in this section. We will continue by writing new and better books, presenting seminars, and publishing *Sew Beautiful* magazine. Most importantly, we will keep trying to work on it with more quality and with more GRACE. How will you become a legend?

God first in all things: Add God to that "RACE" and you achieve GRACE.

> *God loves you. God doesn't want anyone to be hungry*
> *and oppressed. He just puts his big arms around*
> *everybody and hugs them up against himself.*
> —Norman Vincent Peale (1898–1993),
> U.S. cleric and author of *The Power*
> *of Positive Thinking*

Resilience: Get up when you're down. You conquer by continuing.

> *Courage is grace under pressure.*
> —Ernest Hemingway, U.S. author

Action: It is not enough to dream; wake up and work at it!

> *Therefore, prepare your minds for action; be self-*
> *controlled; set your hope fully on the grace to be given*
> *you when Jesus Christ is revealed.*
> —1 Peter 1:13

Creativity: Allow the unusual to happen. It is God who gives us a creative mind and it is OK to use it.

> *There once were some speakers who did not want*
> *to work at their own public relations. Instead, they*

decided to ask the Lord for fast action. They requested
beauty, power, and money.

The Lord answered, "My children, there is beauty
in every atom of your body. I gave it to you the
moment you were conceived. You already have it. All
you need to do is express it. The power of the life force
I gave you the moment you were conceived is switched
on and running. All you need to do is use it. As for
money, I am sorry, but there is none here in heaven. I
only have a superabundance of creative ideas. It is up
to you to catch them and use them."

—Dottie Walters, from her "Speak and
Grow Rich" seminars

Enthusiasm: Allow the spirit of excitement to fill you and spread to your friends. It is contagious and delightfully enriching.

A mediocre idea that generates enthusiasm will go
further than a great idea that inspires no one.

—Mary Kay Ash, founder of Mary Kay
Cosmetics

PART 4

THE PEOPLE

Likability, Loyalty, and Leadership Skills

---

*Getting people to like you is merely
the other side of liking them.*
—Norman Vincent Peale

A Carnegie Foundation study once showed that only 15 percent of a businessperson's success could be attributed to job knowledge and technical skills—an essential element to be sure, but a small overall contribution. It showed that 85 percent of one's success would be determined by what they call "ability to deal with people" and "attitude."

People skills are essential to a successful business. I find that people bent on becoming millionaires are often rather difficult to get along with. Contrary to popular belief, the people I know who are millionaires (and have earned their own wealth) usually are likable in the ways they deal with people, thus creating loyalty with their customers and staff.

In Part 4 we will work on these people skills. I want to share some of my thoughts on communication, sales skills, leadership, problem solving, and ways to be passionate about your business when the honeymoon is over.

CHAPTER TWELVE

Building People Skills: Starting with You

Building rapport with potential customers is an essential ingredient in any business success. Long-term loyalty comes from an excitement about your product and service. Drop the price low enough and a product will be sold to many people; however, you will close your doors. Price does not keep customers loyal to you. Quality and people/service skills build loyalty.

Most of us learned some likability skills growing up, and that is a good start. What if you don't have enough of these skills? Is it hopeless? Absolutely not.

The Difference Between Likable and Unlikable People

When I was in middle school I was miserable! Having now raised my own children, I realize this condition is inherent in the teenage condition. It all began in the seventh grade. I so envied those successful, popular kids of middle school! You know the type, sophisticated and "adult," the ones who have the most pictures in the yearbook, always have a crowd around them, and are gorgeous! I took another look. Actually, many of them were not "gorgeous" in the traditional sense. Hmmmmm. Once that sunk in, I began some serious thinking. It occurred to me, if I could just act like them, I might be as well liked as them.

I became the Agatha Christie of the seventh grade. I lurked in hallways and watched the "legends" in action. It wasn't long before I began to uncover their secrets! They smiled a lot. They talked to everybody. They seemed enthusiastic about everything they did. Even if they were serious students and very smart, they didn't flaunt it. They joined every club and were involved in everything. I had deduced their formula! They had personality and they projected it.

Psychologists have borrowed a word from sewing, *patterning*. It means copying behaviors from others into your life. Now when you sew, if a pattern isn't right, you simply "repattern." Well, I was ready to repattern my life, and now I knew the secrets.

I remember one person in particular upon whom I patterned my likability. She won all of the elections and had the most friends. I had found my role model! I made mental notes of her "patterns." When she walked down the halls at school, she spoke to everyone, trying hard to let them know she genuinely liked them. Her energy and affections were equally spread to rich and poor. She hugged, she joked, she spoke with great enthusiasm to everybody. It was no wonder everybody loved her.

I began to mimic her voice. I noticed her voice was musical, her words went up and down the scale. Mine was monotone and serious—well, what did you expect from a seventh grade sleuth? Her voice almost laughed and sang with every sentence. Her personality was available for all to see.

I made a list of traits of likable people and unlikable people. Likable people are

- positive thinkers
- courteous
- sincere in their caring
- smilers
- personal with people, intimate
- great communicators
- never putting others down
- not demanding, but rather ask politely

- good listeners
- quick to forgive and forget
- enthusiastic about other people and their ideas and abilities
- childlike in their joy of the world
- quick to show appreciation to others for any small kindness

Unlikable people are

- snivelers
- negative thinkers
- sarcastic
- defensive
- quick to point out other people's faults
- insistent that their wishes be carried out, right now
- regularly putting others down
- talkers, and don't know how to listen
- me-oriented
- full of criticism
- nonforgiving
- nonsmilers

So I began to repattern my public personality—to change the amount of energy I gave to everyone I met. Of course, it probably seemed "fake" at first.

I practiced.

I practiced some more.

It became natural, like riding a bike. Suddenly, people began to want to speak to me. It became almost expected that Martha would speak to everyone (especially to the ranks of people whom very few usually spoke to! As a former member of that rank and file, I made sure I put in effort there!)

Then came the senior yearbook. Guess who was elected both "Most Popular" and "Most Likely to Succeed"? I guess the part-time sleuth had learned a thing or two about real Southern hospitality: when you sincerely care about people, they care back.

This section deals with the things I have on my list above, with some suggestions added after a few more years of experience.

As a Man Thinks, So He Shall Become

I enjoy reading the airlines magazines when I fly. They are designed so beautifully and have fun articles. In the October 1995 issue of Delta's *Sky*, there was a nice article about a Georgian, Billy Payne, who is president and chief executive officer of the Atlanta Committee for the Olympic Games. This magazine quoted him as saying, "My father once told me that there will always be people smarter and better than me. But the one thing I could control was my attitude and my work ethic. If I kept a positive attitude and worked harder than the others, I could accomplish a lot."[7]

I have found that my attitude and work ethic changes when I walk with GRACE and choose what I think about. A great mind once said, "You become what you think about."

Through the years, most ancient and modern philosophers have come up with much the same solution to feeling better and getting more done—just tell yourself you can do it.

- Proverbs 23:7 (NKJV)—As he thinks in his heart, so is he.
- Marcus Aurelius—Our life is what our thoughts make it.
- Henry Ford—If you think you can, or you can't, you are right.
- Napoleon Hill—If you can conceive it, and believe it, you can achieve it.

How to Be Likable

Being likable is just a matter of "how to be." It is about GRACE: asking God for guidance, Resilience when people do unlikable things, Actions that will take one closer to being likable,

Creativity in the steps we take to being likable, and Enthusiasm in all the steps we take toward others and our goals.

Be Positive

Every person has sadness and unpleasantness in his/her life. How one handles that unpleasantness is extremely important. I don't care for complaining or to be around people who complain. I certainly hope that I am a caring person when troubles come to other people. There is a difference between sharing a true problem and complaining about anything that happens in one's life.

Complaining does several things:

- makes people want to avoid the complainer
- interrupts relationships and marriages
- ruins parent/child relationships
- ruins adult relationships with their parents
- ruins teacher/student relationships
- ruins business relationships
- gets people fired

If you are a complainer or a whiner, stop! Business success as well as personal success doesn't come to pouters, complainers, and whiners. I do not know *even one* successful person who complains on a regular basis. Successful people call problems "creative challenges." Many of us may have had negative thinking all of our lives from our homes, our schools, our churches, even the weather man! How many times have you heard, "We have a 10 percent chance of rain today." Have you ever heard a weather man praise the possibilities of happiness and say, "Hey there! 90 percent chance of a sunshiny day!"

When someone asks you, "How are you doing?" What do you say?

"Fine. A little tired."

Can you imagine people of passion saying that?! Of course not. But we feed this kind of negativity into ourselves every day!

When someone says to me, "I just can't imagine how things could get much worse," I have to bite my tongue from replying. I can always think of a ton of ways things could get worse!

Find ways to praise the positives. Sometimes they take a bit of creative thinking to find, but just looking for them will help lighten your mood.

Laugh and the world laughs with you;
Weep and you weep alone;
For the sad old earth must borrow its mirth,
But has trouble enough of its own.
—Ella Wheeler Wilcox (1855–1919),
U.S. poet, journalist, *Solitude, st. 1*

Be Uncommonly Courteous

The famous businessman B. C. Forbes (father of Malcolm Forbes) said, "Politeness is the hallmark of the gentle-man and the gentle-woman. No characteristic will so help one to advance, whether in business or society, as politeness. Courtesy is another name for politeness—it costs nothing, but can gain much both for an individual and for an organization."

Think of ways that make the courtesy offered from your company uncommon. Nothing is more persuasive in sales! Although just offering common courtesy consistently is very *uncommon* for most businesses today, think of ways to take it a step further. Saying "Thank you," "You are welcome," and "Please come again" are all ways of offering them common courtesy.

Note the shocked look on the face of your customers when you offer to open a door for them! When was the last time a clerk offered you a chair or a cup of coffee? Sent you a thank-you note? Called you personally to say a new line was in? Just a simple kindness, yet it is absolutely foreign to much of the retail world. Those few businesses that practice it get noticed.

Good manners have much to do with the emotions.
To make them ring true, one must feel them,
not merely exhibit them.
—Amy Vanderbilt (1963),
U.S. hostess, author

That Important Thank-You Note

Each day I take a moment and think, "Who helped to make my way a little easier today?"

Saying thank you is one of the most important parts of a business plan. Everyone appreciates the gesture—it's easy, it helps create intimacy, and, well, it's nice! It is a critical tool for increasing customers' loyalty and sales. I am a firm believer in saying to my customers, "Thank you for buying." You, of course, say it verbally at the time, but there are other ways to say it: a small gift, a handwritten note.

When SECA executives made the decision to put my television show on the national PBS satellite, I was so excited I simply cried. I began to think of an unusual thank-you gift. I purchased two big balloon bouquets just alike and sent each in a large box—it looked like I was shipping a small cow; thank goodness it didn't weigh much!

I keep a stack of thank-you notes close by. It only takes a moment, while I'm on hold on a call, or riding in an airplane, to handwrite a quick thank-you. I have them hand-stamped and mailed the same day. This business principle cannot be overstated enough: Write thank-you cards!

Be Sincere

If I can't truly be sincere in loving customers and really wanting to be friends with them, I should not be in selling. One of the reasons I asked Lilly to help me write this book was my appreciation for a phrase I hear her use over and over as she works with other speakers, "What is the secret of successful speakers? Passion and compassion with a purpose!"[8] Your passion for your work is nothing without compassion for the people God sends into your path. To "be courteous" will surely win you some business. But when you are courteous, and you mean it—when it comes from the inside-out—you will be well on your way! Find ways to speak with kindness, and mean what you say—be sincere!

Selling is not a profession for individuals who are lukewarm about loving people. I enjoy people. I enjoy hearing about their families and seeing their children. I really care about them and their problems. I never bought anything important from an insincere person who seemed to dislike me. There is always another product brand in another store with a genuine salesperson to present it to me in such a way that I enjoy giving my money to her/him.

If you would be loved,
love and be lovable.
—Benjamin Franklin, U.S. statesman,
scientist, and inventor

Be Smiling

I won't hire a salesperson who does not have a readily available smile for customers. I'm not talking about a Pollyanna, silly grin, but a genuine smile. Without feeling welcome, I am not interested in purchasing a product or even in talking with someone about the purchase of a product.

Smiling does not come easily for some people—and they probably don't belong in an industry where you need to sell something. It certainly takes all kinds of people to make the world go round, but all types of people don't make great entrepreneurs. A smile is the quickest way to welcome someone into your territory or into your space.

Every time I have been in a Wal-Mart store, I have been greeted by a smiling individual who said, "Welcome to Wal-Mart" or "Would you like a free sample of . . . ?" They have chosen the best salespeople to be at the checkout counters and they aren't even selling. Or are they? They are selling you on the caring attitude of the whole store. If I have used my charge card or written a check, they usually tell me, "Thank you, Mrs. Pullen. You have a nice day and come back to Wal-Mart." They know enough to read my name off of the check and to call me by name.

Be Intimate

In all of my favorite stores—the ones where I spend the majority of my money—I feel they somehow become an extension of my home. The salespeople treat me the same whether I am dressed in a suit or blue jeans. These stores seem to really like me, which goes a long way in encouraging me to like them. They care whether I am happy with their products. The few times that I needed to take something back, they apologized for the product's not working and for my needing to take the time to bring it back. They never made me feel it was my fault. I feel an intimacy with these businesses.

Making customers feel a part of your family is an important part of intimacy. Letting them know what you think, who you are, who your children are, and what your business stands for is critical in the process of attracting them to you. More importantly, you need to honestly care that all is well in their home, know their children's name, their spouses.

Creating an intimate business relationship with your customers takes a great deal of work. But when you create a client base characterized by closeness of friendship, you create a loyal and solid base upon which to build your business. Soon you will begin to count your friends among your clients. This kind of intimacy can only occur by diligent effort and study of what they want out of life. You will find the skill you most need to be intimate is to be inquiring.

Be Inquiring

Dottie Walters, world famous speaker and businesswoman, once told me that one of the main keys to her success was to be more interested than interesting. She illustrated it with the story of the great actress Sarah Bernhardt. Late in Sarah's career, when her theatrical company arrived at a new city, a newspaper editor told a young reporter to go out to interview her.

He didn't want to go. He said, "She is an old has-been!"

When he came back, he flew to his typewriter and excitedly wrote a glowing story about Sarah for his newspaper.

The savvy editor asked the young man, "What did you and Sarah Bernhardt talk about?"

He replied, "Come to think of it, she didn't say much. But every time I said something, she leaned forward with a smile, looked into my eyes, and said, 'And then?'"

Ego is a wonderful thing. It helps you to be proud of those things you have a right to be proud of. But a delicate ego is a sign of a person who is not walking with GRACE. A person with a delicate ego thinks he or she must be interesting, rather than interested—a fatal mistake in someone who is likable. Instead, be inquiring and invite your listener to communicate with you.

EGO = Edging, God, Out
—Ken Blanchard, U.S. businessman
and business management author

Be Inviting

Would you like customers to flood your place of business? Did you invite them in? No, I don't mean an ad in the paper or a form letter. I mean, did you call and say, "Now, ya'll come on over this Saturday for a cookie and see our new stuff!" (That's not bad grammar; we talk that way in Huntsville.) By the way, ya'll means "you all," and that is exactly who I want to come in my doors if I am in business. I want all of the people! When they walk in the door, do you invite them to come and see the new items? When they are about to leave, do you invite them to come back soon? If you have new products, call and enthusiastically invite your best customers to learn more about them.

Be Enthusiastic

I have never met a successful person—from billionaire to baton twirler—who was not enthusiastic. Stanford University did a study that showed that during a sale, 15 percent of the success was due to product knowledge, and 85 percent was credited to enthusiasm!

Enthusiasm is a keen, animated interest, an absorbing or controlling possession of the mind by any subject, interest, or pursuit. That is what the dictionary will tell you. But look deeper! Enthusiasm is so much more. Do you know the word *enthusiasm* comes from the Greek *entheos*? Originally it meant people who were so filled with God (*theos*) as to seem inspired.

Today the expression has lost its religious meaning to most of the world. But anyone who has been filled with the joy of enthusiasm knows that passionate elevation of the soul as you fill with a joyous spirit of GRACE. In my life I know this spirit of enthusiasm is a gift from God—a gift that is all the more wonderful in that it keeps filling up those around me. We are not here on this planet simply to exist, but to live, and to live abundantly. Once you tap into what makes you enthusiastic, work on ways to use your enthusiasm in all aspects of your business life.

The real secret of success is enthusiasm. Yes, more than enthusiasm, I would say excitement. I like to see men get excited. When they get excited they make a success of their lives.

—Walter Percy Chrysler (1875–1940), American automobile manufacturer who founded the Chrysler Corporation in 1925

Be Childlike

Most of us have been conditioned to act subdued and restrained in our dealings. We have effectively been robbed of our natural, childlike enthusiasm. Can you think of anything as attractive as the wonderful energy created by a child who is filled with enthusiasm? A five-year-old child laughs five hundred times a day. By the time we are adults we laugh only about fifteen times a day. Who made this rule? Who said that it is not "adult" to fill yourself with delight and joy?

The word *delight* comes from the Latin word *del-lacere*, meaning "to allure." How interesting that being filled with childlike delight is also alluring.

> *In things relating to enthusiasm, no man is sane who does not know how to be insane on proper occasions.*
> —Henry Ward Beecher (1813–1987),
> U.S. clergyman, writer, and
> newspaper editor

How to Discover Your Personal Enthusiasms

A friend of mine, Dr. Dennis O'Nan, opened new avenues in my heart concerning enthusiasm. He said, "Martha, look at the last four letters of the word *enthusiasm*: i-a-s-m. I like to say they stand for 'I Am Sold Myself.'" I understood!

For instance, I am absolutely enthusiastic about sewing. I love it. I get excited about it. If someone with just a little interest in sewing asks me about it, I can easily sell them on the joy of it, the sisterhood of the people involved, the passion, the history, the . . . I can sell you on the benefits of sewing because "I am sold myself." Let's put the shoe on the other foot, however, and take another person's hobby, such as baseball card collecting. Could I have enthusiasm for that? Could I sell others on the purchase of baseball cards? I probably couldn't because I don't love baseball cards, nor frankly the game of baseball. The things I can convert others to are things I am sold on, like doing mission work with my church.

We need to find our God-given talents and concentrate on sharing them with others.

Enthusiasm. To find it in ourselves we must look at the word: *ethos*, "from God." First it is the Spirit filling our souls from God, then "I Am Sold Myself" ends the word. With a combination of these two ideas, enthusiasm is the greatest quality on earth.

So we must learn how to utilize enthusiasm in order to move into that exciting and creative segment of the human race—the achievers. You will find among them total agreement that enthusiasm is the priceless ingredient of personality that helps to achieve happiness and self-fulfillment.
—Norman Vincent Peale (1898–1993),
U.S. cleric, author of *The Power of Positive Thinking*

Dottie Walters puts it another way, "Go beyond simmering, even to boiling, and you will discover talents and powers you never dreamed were yours."

CHAPTER THIRTEEN

Communication Skills

Practically synonymous with people skills is good communication skills. Communication is the key to winning, and more importantly, keeping customers. Without good communication skills, a business won't make it.

Most adults aren't completely equipped with perfect communication skills; luckily, communication skills can be improved. In this section we'll talk about listening, communicating your successes without seeming conceited, personality types, magic phrases of language, and how to make your customers feel important.

Don't Tell: Ask and Listen

I believe the best selling skills in the world are helping your prospects see the value of your product through politeness and the ability to listen to their needs and desires. Using questions effectively is one of the best ways to be able to listen to another person's thoughts.

When we were working on opening our Canadian market, part of the Canadian team of a large sewing machine company was enthusiastically talking to us about some new ventures together. The managing director was interested in having his top executives listen to our plan, but I don't think he was truly sold on using heirloom sewing as a marketing tool. They had a dinner meeting for us with their top management. I asked, and listened, "Tell me what is happening in sewing in Canada? Where are your most successful areas? Least successful? Do you have any feeling why one is successful and the other is not? Are you teaching classes in your dealerships? Why (or why not)? Where would you see our seminars being most successful? Where would we start if we were to choose to begin opening up Canada? Would you like to hear about the items we sell that you could import for you and your dealers? Tell me about your business. . . . "

After listening carefully for most of the dinner, I began to understand their needs and their current situation. We discussed how we might help them sell more sewing machines, as well as train their dealers to do the same thing. We got the deal.

The essence of selling has nothing to do with telling people how wonderful you are. It has everything to do with listening to the prospective customer and finding out his/her needs in relationship to the goods you have to deliver.

Signs of a Bad Listener

- interrupts the customers while they are speaking
- talks over someone
- finishes sentences for others
- talks more than the other person
- doesn't establish eye contact with the person who is talking
- looks around the room to see who else is there while someone is talking to him/her

Signs of a Good Listener

- hears the message behind the words and deciphers the true needs
- uses gentle questions to explore and question, then watches carefully, asks the appropriate question, and listens again
- later ties what they have heard into the idea they are trying to communicate
- takes notes, and writes down key points that are important to the customer
- smiles
- establishes eye contact (keeps smiling)

- nods his/her head up and down
- repeats key concepts back to the customer
- is often silent (Often your silence will be thought of as brilliant and wise and will encourage others to communicate.)

Conceit, Pride, Image, and Success

It is often a fine line to walk between asking careful questions, listening carefully, and still letting the prospect know you have the best product available. People are attracted to success; they want good services and products. But we are repelled by bragging and conceit. So, how do you tell them you are rather wonderful without appearing conceited?

At the beginning of the meeting with our Canadian colleagues, I said lightheartedly that I was traveling almost as much as I could stand and that I wasn't looking for another job. I didn't want them to think that I *needed* jobs traveling and teaching. The only way that kind of statement works, said in a lighthearted manner or not, is if you have built up enough of your own successes that it is true.

Communication and Personality Types

Brilliant communicators seem to have the ability to read people and communicate in a way they hear and understand. Through the millennia, "sages" have been trying to analyze people and categorize them by personality type. Most have found that people divide nicely into four distinct groups. Even ancient Babylonians saw the natural divide of personality types and divided all peoples into earth, wind, water, and fire. As science has advanced, many other studies have been conducted. Below is an overview of a few of them.

- Hermes Trismegistus, or Thoth: Earth, Wind, Water, and Fire—Astrology
- Dr. Carl Jung, 1930: Thinker, Intuitor, Feeler, Sensor (Jung developed the introvert concept.)

- Dr. John Geier, University of Minnesota: DISC—Dominant, Inspirational, Steady, Compliant
- David W. Merril and Roger Reid: Amiable, Analytical, Expressive, Driver
- Myers-Briggs: Extroversion-Introversion, Sensing-Intuition, Thinking-Feeling, Judging-Perceptive
- Albert Mehrabian: Domineering, Submissive, Pleasant, Unpleasant (There are two levels of each, for a total of eight types.)
- Jim Cathcart and Tony Alessandra: Director, Relater, Socializer, Thinker.

After reading these, I developed my own little system!

Communicating with Dominant Doris or Donald

As I have dealt with dominant people I have learned a few things. Dominant people don't smile a lot at first. They wear power clothing and very little jewelry. What is power clothing? Plain, dark colors, tailored, and not too "in" seem to best describe dominant clothing. Jewelry is simple and usually it is real gold. Hair is usually simple and not very modish. Conservative is the general rule for the dominant Doris and Donald. When shaking hands with dominant people, they will usually turn your hand toward the bottom. They don't like to be too close to you physically. Probably the same thing holds true emotionally. Their sales demonstration needs to be quick, professional, and businesslike. They don't like the "good old boy" style of selling. Don't waste his/her time with silly talk or chatter. Get to the point. Dominant people usually drive red or black status cars. If the product is a machine, they will want to know how fast it runs since they are very driven and fast people. They usually like the top of the line and other status features of a product. Point that out. Make their demonstration short because they "don't have time" to stick around. They think they are the "busiest" people in the world and you might acknowledge that fact to them.

Communicating with Enthusiastic Emma or Ernie

Enthusiasm abounds in this type of person. They are great salespeople themselves and they expect you to put a lot of energy into your presentation. To discover if you have an enthusiastic person on your hands, look for several characteristics. They smile a lot and wear lots of jewelry. Their clothing is stylish as well as their hairstyle. They usually conceal any gray hair. They look youthful and they act the same. They love fast machines and fashionable anything. They are intrigued by creativity in a product and they don't want too many instructions. Make their presentation interesting, quick, and upbeat. Don't get into lengthy explanations about the warranty and the longevity of the product because they will probably forget to send in the warranty card anyway. Longevity isn't of the utmost importance because they will want the latest model as soon as it is on the market. Your place of business needs to be stylish and friendly. You need to smile and tell them how wonderful the product is and how much everyone wants it. If there is any "show biz" associated with the product, for goodness sake tell them about it.

Communicating with Sweet Sue or Seth

Sue and Seth are home-loving, family-oriented people and they are unique. Their clothing isn't too expensive and is usually not overly stylish. Usually they smile softly and they aren't loud people. Their hair is styled in a natural way, usually not colored to hide gray hair. Their favorite topic is their children or grandchildren and everything associated with them. They always have lots of pictures of their family, and if you want to sell them anything you need to look carefully at the complete book of pictures that they carry. You need to ask the children's names, what grade they are in, what their interests are, what sports or hobbies they have, and anything else you can think of concerning the children. You need to listen as they answer all of the questions. They usually drive older model vans or station wagons. At least one of their cars is old and they are saving cash to purchase their next one. They like baby blue, gray, or white cars, and they rarely ever speed.

Sue and Seth love to tell about their family matters. Sue loves to tell you what she cooked for supper last night, and Seth loves to tell you about the family plans for the weekend. They sometimes carry a copy of their children's report cards in their purses or briefcases, and you had better act interested if they bring them out.

They always consult with their husband or wife before making major financial decisions. They usually think about a purchase before buying it and they try not to use credit cards or financing. If you have financing, it would be best if you can provide a ninety-days-same-as-cash plan. If you have a video presentation available, give it to them because they probably will watch it. They prefer quality products that last; therefore, they like warranties. Many times they do not purchase the top of the line. Always give them a choice of products and do not push toward a purchase.

I think it is most important to establish intimacy with this type of person and always let them come back over and over to see the product. Assure them of lessons on how to use the product if applicable. I have sent the product home for them to try on occasion. Always invite them to spend a lot of time in your business trying it out.

Do not push these individuals. They make very careful decisions and they will never come back if they are pushed. They are loyal customers and usually will favor one brand. It is a good day if that brand is yours. Be patient in selling to them.

Communicating with Mathematical Mary or Martin

Some people are just born engineers. It doesn't matter if they studied engineering or not; they just act mathematical. They don't smile easily and are usually suspicious of those who smile a lot. Don't get too close to them physically and don't be too "down-home." They aren't loud and don't want to attract attention to themselves. They are a bit suspicious of anyone who tries to sell to them. They will do research on any product and probably will carry a consumer's guide around in a pocket. They dress conservatively and usually not in a very stylish mode. They drive conservative cars and are very careful about spending their money. They are proud of the fact that their foreign car gets thirty-eight miles to the gallon and has 248,000 miles so far. They are sensitive individuals, although you might not know it upon first meeting them. They don't like change. You will have to spend time to sell them anything. They certainly won't buy if the product isn't a good value. Determining what value they want is a skill you will have to develop.

They always want to read all of the contract and the warranty. They don't sign anything until they have studied every word. If the product is mechanical, you had better know about the engineering features of the inside of the machine. They like good machinery.

Decisions sometimes make them uneasy, and they will come to your business over and over again. Please be patient with them and they will probably come back enough times to feel comfortable making a decision with you.

Magic Phrases of Language

The difference between the right word and the almost right word is the difference between lightning and the lightning bug.
—Mark Twain, U.S. author, humorist

A number of years ago, I thought I wanted to be a school counselor. Consequently I enrolled in a graduate course at the University of Georgia. That summer I found out that I talk too much to be an effective counselor; however, the skills I learned that summer have been the cornerstone of some of my selling success as well as managing success.

There are many phrases that can trigger negative or positive responses. I call those that trigger positive responses my "magic phrases." These magic phrases help me build confidence and trust with people. For instance, "Too busy" is the most excuse-oriented phrase I know. It's grossly overused and really means "I don't want to," or "I'm maladjusted and can't organize my time well enough to do ten things at once." We are never too busy to undertake the things that are important to us personally or professionally.

If I don't want to do something, I could say, "I don't want to do that." Usually I soften the blow by saying, "Interesting idea, but not for me just now. My focus is on other projects." In a business I might adjust that to "At this time, I don't think that fits into our objectives." If I don't want to make time for a new project, but I think it will fit into our scheme, I say, "I think that might be a good idea. I will speak with my staff and see who will be the best person to undertake this task."

Here are some charts with more magic phrases:

Don't Say . . .	Because They Hear . . .	Do Say . . .
"I'm sorry, that's all I can do."	"I'm not interested in taking any effort for you!"	"Please tell me, what else may I do?"
"Can I help you?"	(It makes them think, "I dunno, can you?")	"What can I help you find today?"
"Thank you for holding."	(They are already annoyed because they had to hold; don't remind them!)	"I'm sorry, thank you for being patient."
"We can't."	"We don't want to."	"We will."
"I'll try."	"I will put it as my least priority."	"I will."
"I don't know."	"I don't care."	"I will find out."
"I'm sorry, there is nothing I can do."	"I'm not sorry, there is nothing I want to do to help you."	"Let me find a way to fix this situation."
""If we have those, they're on the shelf."	"You are not important to me; go shop someplace else."	"Those should be on aisle four. I will show you."

Don't Say . . .	Because They Hear . . .	Do Say . . .
"Who's calling?"	"You are most likely not important enough to speak to important people like us."	"May I tell John who is calling?"
"There is nobody here I can ask right now."	"I am an idiot, and we are an inefficient company that has no idea what it's doing. Call somebody else."	"Let me have your phone number. We want to find that answer for you!"

Magic Phrases for Communicating in Conflict

Keep these phrases close to the surface of your mind so they will be ready when you need them!

- It seems to me . . .
- I am of the opinion . . .
- You might want to consider . . .
- Have you given consideration to . . . ?
- When you do (or say) that, it makes me feel . . .

"It seems to me"

. . . is the first of my magic phrases. When I want someone to really listen to me, I use these words before I make a statement. Remember that facts aren't facts to all people. Many times a fact is true only to me and if I want someone to listen to my opinion, I need to preface it with, "It seems to me" rather than, "You know something or the other is true." The words "It seems to me" are nonthreatening and possibly will cause another person to really hear what I am trying to say.

This phrase relays that you are looking at a statement not in a black-and-white, absolute way but rather in an open way. Even when I want to add, "but you know that this is true," I refrain if I want to have the other individual give consideration to my thinking.

Let me give an example of how a potential customer might react to two different approaches of presenting facts. If the salesperson is trying to sell a Ford automobile, he/she can say, "This is the best automobile in the whole world." If the customer absolutely agrees with him/her, then this statement is a great statement. However, what if the customer is looking at a Ford, a Volvo, and a Chrysler? The statement about the Ford being the best automobile might not be true for that customer. If the salesperson wants the customer to really listen to his sales presentation about Ford, he/she should say, "It seems to me that Ford is the best made automobile available on today's market, and I would like the opportunity to share with you why I have found this to be true." Now, the customer is nonthreatened and possibly will want to hear about the Ford and its wonderful features.

Pronouncing "absolute truth" is bad communication in almost any situation but especially in the world of sales and management of other people. "Truth" always says that I am right and that you may be wrong. I believe that both sides lose when this happens. By using "it seems to me," you can pronounce your "truth" without it being seen as anything but *your* "truth." That way another person might be more inclined to consider your opinion.

"I am of the opinion"

. . . is another one of my magic phrases to be used when one's opinion is stated. One of the greatest turnoffs to me is someone's making a statement such as, "You know that this product is the best one available." Actually, I don't know any such fact, and my thinking might be that another product is absolutely the best one. To state my thinking on a product and to have the customer at least listen to my opinion, I need to state, "I am of the opinion that this product is the very best one for the job." Once again, I haven't pronounced "truth" to another person, and he/she might be able to listen to my ideas with an open mind.

"You might want to consider"

. . . is an excellent way of suggesting that an individual look at your product for purchase. Once again, don't say, "You will love this product," because you can't state with certainty that someone will love anything. That is up to the individual purchasing the product to decide.

"Have you given consideration to?"

. . . is another way of using "you might want to consider" but rather stating it in question form, which is one of my favorite ways of selling anything. Answers might vary from, "Well, no, I haven't thought of it in that way" to, "Yes, I have thought about it."

"When you do that, it makes me feel"

. . . is another great statement to learn when one wants to have better communication skills. This communicates what a behavior does to a person rather than what the person does to a person. It is a lot easier to accept that my behavior is not pleasing to another than to accept that I am not pleasing to another person. Instead of "Now, that's a dumb thing to do," I would say, "When you do that, it makes me feel that I don't understand what you intended." I have not criticized another's statements or behaviors but rather told how they made me feel. The communication lines are still open, and I haven't offended the other person.

Some other magic phrases to ease you through conflict and build bridges are:

- I hear your concern.
- I see what you are saying.
- I understand your point.
- You're right.
- I really hadn't thought of that.
- Tell me more.
- That is really an interesting idea. I wonder if we might also consider . . .

> *No matter how busy you are, you must take time to*
> *make the other person feel important.*
> —Mary Kay Ash, founder,
> Mary Kay Cosmetics

The Most Magic Phrase in Communication

What set of words do we like to hear above all others? Why, our own names! Whenever you are trying to build a relationship, get the person's name as quickly as possible, and use it often in the conversation. This establishes intimacy quickly. My suggestion is to use Mr. or Mrs. until told to do otherwise. When people call me Dr. Pullen or Mrs. Pullen, I quickly say, "Oh, please call me Martha, everybody does."

In Europe, there is a custom that one never calls an individual by his or her first name until that person gives you his or her first name. In every situation I think each person must size up what to call customers. When I opened my first retail store, I always referred to customers who were older than I as Mrs. So-and-So. Those who were my age or younger, I usually called by the first name. If there were any doubt, I always used Mrs.

In my husband's dental office, he introduces himself to new patients as Joe Pullen. Everyone who comes into that dental office probably knows that he is Dr. Pullen. He has always felt that the title Dr. distances himself from his patients. He and his staff refer to their patients as Mr. or Mrs. unless they request his calling them by their first name.

I have been in a few physicians' offices where they called me by my first name before I even walked back to the examining area. I am offended. I am also offended when physicians call me "Martha" yet introduce themselves as Dr. So and So. I absolutely know that they are a Dr. or I wouldn't have come for medical advice. It seems that the better versed and more newly trained physicians know to greet patients by saying "Hello,

Mrs. Pullen, I'm Tom Drake." What does not establish intimacy to me is "Hello, Martha, I'm Dr. Drake." The last time that happened to me, I replied, "Hello, Dr. Drake, I'm Dr. Pullen."

> *Let your conversation be always full*
> *of grace, seasoned with salt.*
> —Colossians 4:6a

How to Be a Legendary Salesperson

To be a legendary success in sales, you must have the qualities we discussed in the previous section on likability and loyalty. Those are only part of the big picture. A business is not a business until something is sold. I have found some specific skills and wonderful techniques that bring a customer to say "yes." These skills aren't necessarily born into a person; they can be learned. Although I began formal study of both management and marketing after opening my business, my teaching career was the ultimate in management, marketing, and selling. Have you ever tried to sell Shakespeare to a twelfth-grader during the spring quarter before graduation?

In this section I want to share some step-by-step strategies that may help your customer say "yes."

Martha's Twelve Commandants of Successful Selling

1. Recognize that your customers are smart and special.
2. Have a good product.
3. Know your product well.
4. *Love* your product!
5. Take care of your old customers.
6. Wear a smile and give it away to everyone.
7. Think positively and successfully.
8. Never complain or use negative words.
9. Become a wonderful listener.
10. Ask for the order.

11. Always do more than is expected of you.
12. Sell with GRACE.

Make Each Customer Feel Important

Where do you prefer to shop? Think of the places you don't go anymore. Ask yourself "why?" Is it their attitude and the way they deal with you? It usually comes down to that for me.

When I started my first store, I would look each person right in the eye and convey from the inside-out how glad I was to see him or her—and they kept coming back! I found it important to hire employees who had the same skill of enthusiastically welcoming people as they walked through the door.

Use Questions to Sell

Ask questions! They can be inspiring. During a sales presentation, don't just tell about the product; ask at least fifteen questions. Let them answer the questions. People don't argue with their own data, but they can and do argue with yours. Joseph Joubert, a French moralist, said, "We can convince others by our own arguments, but we can only persuade them by their own." Or as Ben Franklin said, "A man convinced against his will is of the same opinion still."

Ask questions that will open up the conversation. Try these:

- "Are you looking for a particular color?"
- "Are you interested in our current specials?"
- "How might you use _____?"
- "What have you heard about _____?"
- "What is it you don't like about _____?"
- "How would it be useful?"
- "What has been your experience with it before?"
- "Is the reputation of the company you are dealing with important to you?" (This can help you elevate yourself above the competition.)

- "What most interests you about _____?"
- "How familiar are you with _____?"
- "What great things have you heard about (our company) or (our product)?"
- "What brought you in today?"
- "What can I do to help you?"
- "Where may I direct you?"
- "How may we be of assistance?"
- "What did you like most about what you are currently using, driving, etc.?"
- "What do you dislike about what you are currently using?"
- "What can we do to make this work better?"
- "What key results are you looking for?"

If I were in furniture store sales, during a demonstration of a recliner or mattress, I might try these sorts of questions:

- "Did you know that Scotchgard really protects the upholstery?"
- "Have you ever seen an easier reclining chair mechanism?"
- "Have you slept on a more comfortable mattress?"
- "Did you know that the average mattress lasts thirty years?"
- "I wonder if you know that our company has a warranty of thirty years?"
- "Have you ever thought about the fact that you spend 56 of the 168 hours of your week in bed?"
- "How important do you think a good night's sleep is to the rest of your life and health?"

Step by Step to Get to "Yes"

This step-by-step system will show you how to be nice, intimate, inquiring, and inviting. In many of the following twelve steps, remember to write down their answers while they talk.

This is active listening and is very flattering. I call this process, "pencil listening."

1. Discover the person's needs by asking.
2. Practice active listening—ask questions about your customers' needs and *write down their answers.*
3. Be genuinely interested in the other person.
4. Small-talk to gather information about their life. Ask about children or grandchildren.
5. Share something about your family, church, hunting trips, fishing trips, or other hobbies, but use these as a method to get them talking about themselves.
6. Be organized in what you want to communicate (your product, concept, idea, etc.).
7. Be enthusiastic about what you want to communicate.
8. Be confident that yours is the best.
9. If they bring up "the competition," praise the competition's products and/or ideas. End the praise by telling them why you think yours is the best and is worthy of their consideration.
10. Learn the magic phrases of communication.
11. Look the customer in the eye. Never stare at the floor.
12. Ask for the order.

My greatest strength as a consultant is to be ignorant and ask a few questions.
—Peter Drucker, author and speaker, considered the father of modern management principles

---

Get Business in Your Door through Your Phone

Making thank-you phone calls is another way to win friends and influence people. Making solicitation phone calls is more difficult. To turn your hobby into profit, you must overcome phone fear. So many of us freeze when it is time to pick up the phone and call a prospect.

How does one overcome phone fear? Simply by planning the whole conversation. Organize your thoughts before you call, make a list of what you want to say, then say it. Have your plan in mind if you want to talk business with someone and make an appointment to present a product. Here are the steps I suggest you take to make your calling a bit easier:

- Identify main prospects (at least twenty). Write down their telephone numbers.
- Ask your core customers to give you at least three names who would be good prospects.
- Decide if they would be good prospects. Choose the top five out of that twenty.
- Call at least five people per day. (Remember, they can only say no. If you know these people, they probably won't mind your calling.)
- Take your product to their house if they can't come to your business.
- Make an appointment if you are going to the customer rather than the customer coming to you. *Don't cold call.*
- If you are going to make an appointment, preface it with, "I have two things to ask you and it will only take two minutes of your time. I know you are busy."

Resilience in the Legendary Salesperson

For every five well-thought-out good prospects you contact, four will say "no," at least temporarily. Leave the four "no's" smiling. Leave the doors open. Be thankful for the one person who is waiting for you because you have the answer to his or her problem.

Sometimes it takes twenty prospects to reach the four sales, and all four come in the last five people. It is a matter of odds.

To get the odds going in your direction, you must take the initiative to speak to twenty prospects. The results will be four sales, and sixteen callbacks because . . .

If you try, you may not win every time.
If you don't try at all,
you will never win. Guaranteed.
—Dottie Walters, author and speaker

CHAPTER FOURTEEN

How to Be a Legendary Leader

I only have one real talent. I hire the best people in the world. That is the true secret of my success. All business involves teamwork. No person ever built a successful business by him/herself.

Ray Kroc, founder of McDonald's, is said to have explained it as follows: "A well-run restaurant is like a winning baseball team; it makes the most of every crew member's talent and takes advantage of every split-second opportunity to speed up service."

There is no business until something is sold. Nothing moves until your people make it happen. Vince Lombardi, coach of the Green Bay Packers, is known to have said, "The achievements of an organization are the result of the combined efforts of each individual."

The essence of entrepreneurship is being a charismatic leader as well as a worker since the owner must pretty well do everything in the beginning. Actually, fifteen years into my business, I still do some of those beginning tasks. Mostly I am only the guide, as well as an equal worker. One simply must know how to manage. These skills can be learned through continuing education, enrolling in college courses, reading books from the library, and taking seminars.

In this section I have a few thoughts for you on how to hire good people, heart management, building up team morale, bottom-up management, delegation, setting wages, using your family as your work team, and when to fire team members.

Take away my people, but leave my factories,
and soon grass will grow on the factory floor.
Take away my factories, but leave my people,
and soon we will have a new and better factory!

—Andrew Carnegie (1835–1919), poor
boy born in Scotland, who became a
dominant figure in the U.S. steel
industry, an industrialist, and a
philanthropist

Hire Good People

One of my favorite business quotations is "No man is an island" from John Donne. None of us stands alone in business. My staff helps me in the vision, the implementation, and the evaluation. They are the greatest!

Traits of the Top Performers on My Team

I am blessed with a great team. God has sent certain people to me who do more than they are asked. They nearly always say "I can," not "I'm just too busy." They uplift others on the team. They create new ideas for the company and help implement them. They are always polite to others on the team and to consumers. They are positive thinkers, not gripers. They are not lazy. They aren't afraid to pick up the heavy suitcases and to vacuum the floor.

Tips on Hiring Good People

- Ask your current employees and associates for ideas. Often others close to you, who know your strengths and weaknesses, will have great ideas.
- Take the time to create a qualifications checklist before you hire someone. This will help you determine areas in

which the applicants are strong and weak. If you do decide to hire an individual, this information will be valuable for training purposes.

- Your initial impression of the candidate is critical, especially in situations like sales, customer service, and management where a great deal of interpersonal interaction is the mainstay of the position. Remember, your customers will be making the same quick judgment.

- Don't get so excited talking about your business that you don't get the applicants talking. You need to find out about them; they don't need to know much about you.

- Use open-ended questions in your interview. If you ask a question like "We are looking for someone who is outgoing and enthusiastic; are you outgoing and enthusiastic?" he will of course say yes. A better question would be "What two adjectives best describe you?"

- If you are planning on using the person as a salesperson, customer service person, or telephone receptionist, his or her written responses will mean very little to you. Your main concern is how she sounds. If your customer never sees her, then do your entire interview by phone.

- Make your hiring decisions with GRACE.

Never be associated with someone you can't be proud of, whether you work for him or he works for you.
—Victor Kiam,
CEO and President of
Remington Products

Heart Management

By *heart management*, I mean treating individuals on your team with the utmost respect as God's creations—an ideal you come closer to when you lead your team with GRACE.

Praise

As a school teacher and later as a college professor, I found that praise got better results than criticism. The more I encouraged my students and sang their praises, the more they performed. Giving a student an opportunity to get extra credit after a bad test grade did more than saying, "Sorry, Bud. You just didn't study."

Praise means praising even the smallest improvement of an employee who really isn't doing as well as you would like. Praise means remembering to praise the employee who is your star and who is paid better than all the rest. Pay is one method of praise but not the only one. I simply don't know of a business that can afford to always pay the most effective employee better than all of the rest, no matter what level. I have found praise among employees, rather than criticism, to be a great motivator to work harder.

Wars may be fought with weapons, but they are won by men. It is the spirit of men who follow and of the man who leads that gains the victory.

—General George Smith Patton, Jr. (1885–1945), American general. During World War II he commanded the 3rd Army, which spearheaded the liberation of France (1944) and the defeat of Germany (1945).

Expect Greatness

We awaken in others the same attitude of mind we hold towards them.

—Elbert Hubbard (1856–1915), U.S. author

People will perform well if you expect them to perform well and then praise them for it. I have high expectations of my employees. I have heard that John Steinbeck said, "It is the nature of man to rise to greatness, if greatness is expected of them."

My team is sometimes overworked. We all need more people to do our jobs.

My team is paid fairly.

My team accomplishes the impossible many times during the year.

I expect from my team the kind of results no sane employer would have the gall to ask for.

I think most people don't realize their greatness. The most wonderful gift you can offer anyone is to see them as what they can only fantasize about. Then you must know that this person is capable of accomplishing this greatness. Once they learn how good they really are, they will not easily settle for their old standards.

When I was a high school student, we needed new curtains in the home economics department. Our teacher, Mrs. Ingram, called me and a few classmates together and explained which windows needed curtains. She told us that we had a small budget to buy material and rods and gave us permission to go to The Mill Ends Store to purchase the needed goods. We had no idea how to measure for curtains, make curtains, buy material, buy rods, or install rods. When I boldly asked, "Mrs. Ingram, how do we do all of this?" she quietly thought a few minutes and answered, "Girls, just do it."

Mrs. Ingram believed we could make those draperies, and she flatly refused to take the responsibility she had given to us. Guess what? We did it! A lesson that was never forgotten. She knew we could do it—so we believed her.

Practice What You Preach

Telling employees to pitch in whenever a job needs to be done is a far cry from them seeing you pitch in. I take my turn running the vacuum cleaner, emptying the trash, and cleaning the bathrooms. I don't expect my team to do anything that I don't do myself. Likewise, the leader who is the last to arrive in the morning and the first to leave at night can expect the same from his or her team. I wish I could tell you I am a model of the best a person could be—I can't. But, with God's help, I am sincerely working at being better today than I was yesterday. My team believes that I am becoming the best, and I believe they are becoming the best. As a good leader, demonstrate a work ethic that says, "I will be better at this task today than I was yesterday! I will have a responsibility and accountability for all tasks within our company."

Sermons We See

I'd rather see a sermon than hear one any day;
I'd rather one should walk with me
than merely tell the way
The eye's a better pupil and more willing than the ear,
Fine counsel is confusing, but example's always clear;
And the best of all the preachers
are the men who live their creeds,
For to see good put in action is what everybody needs.
I soon can learn to do it if you'll let me see it done;
I can watch your hands in action,
but your tongue too fast may run.
And the lecture you deliver may be very wise and true,
But I'd rather get my lessons by observing what you do;
For I might misunderstand you
and the high advice you give,
But there's no misunderstanding
how you act and how you live.
When I see a deed of kindness, I am eager to be kind.
When a weaker brother stumbles
and a strong man stays behind
Just to see if he can help him,
then the wish grows strong in me

To become as big and thoughtful
as I know that friend to be.
And all travelers can witness
that the best of guides to-day
Is not the one who tells them,
but the one who shows the way.
One good man teaches many,
men believe what they behold;
One deed of kindness noticed is worth forty that are told.
Who stands with men of honor
learns to hold his honor dear,
For right living speaks a language
which to every one is clear.
Though an able speaker charms me with his eloquence,
I say, I'd rather see a sermon than to hear one, any day.
—Edgar A. Guest (1881)

Never Take Credit, Give It

I never heard of Coach Bear Bryant's saying, "I am a great coach," yet he, in my opinion, was one of the most wonderful men who ever lived. If only there were millions like him. He taught values to his players, and one of the most valuable lessons attributed to him is: When everything goes bad say, "I did it." When things go in an average or mediocre way say, "We did it." When things go especially wonderfully say, "They did it."

Giving other people credit for successes is absolutely necessary in my leadership philosophy. Taking full credit when anything goes wrong is always my leadership responsibility. Everybody makes mistakes, and the buck stops with me when any in my organization make a mistake. I take the blame when things go wrong and I praise my employees when we are successful. When people say, "Martha, you do so many wonderful things and I don't see how you do it all," I reply, "My staff is wonderful! They make me look good."

Lead from the Bottom-Up

We hire the best people and let them be their own boss, most of the time. Our management is bottom-up, and each member of the team designs her own time within our framework. Nobody breathes down anyone else's neck and there is almost no criticism of an employee's work. Occasionally I give employees a list of tasks; however, my preferred way is to let each employee plan his/her own job around the general job/task description. I let them participate in performance goals and deadlines.

> *When people are highly motivated,*
> *it's easy to accomplish the impossible.*
> *And when they're not,*
> *it's impossible to accomplish the easy.*
> —Bob Collings

Build Up Your Employees

It is much easier to hire great people than to try and make them great. But if you don't continue to build them up, they will either leave you or not offer you their willing and exceptional performance. Here are some things I do to build up my team.

- Never criticize. Gently offer suggestions for improvement without anger or ridicule.
- Overlook what can be overlooked.
- Treat everybody like valued adults.
- Understand family needs.
- Give flexible vacations and paid leave.
- Meet real emergencies with special considerations.
- Allow for interest in employees' family and faith.
- Lighten up! Humor helps. John Morreall, a famous humor researcher, said that the "value . . . of humor in the workplace . . . is its fostering of family of traits and activities

that include a tolerance for novelty, ambiguity, and change; divergent thinking, creative problem solving, and risk taking. I call these collectively 'mental flexibility.'"[9]
- Have a few parties . . .
  - Christmas
  - birthdays
  - farewell
  - occasional hamburger cookout in the back parking lot
  - anytime anyone wants to bring something special to eat and share

---

A cheerful heart is good medicine,
but a crushed spirit dries up the bones.
—Proverbs 17:22

The Art of Delegation

Surround yourself with the best people you can find,
delegate authority, and don't interfere.
—Ronald Reagan (b. 1911),
U.S. Republican politician,
former U.S. president

For years I had difficulty delegating. I created ironclad myths, lies, and legends to justify my own attitude:

- Martha is the only person who knows how to do this!
- The phone call won't be as effective if Martha doesn't make it!
- Martha must know absolutely everything about the financial side of this business!
- Martha must be the main writer in all of her sewing books or it won't really be hers!
- Martha must always go to the consumer markets because the sales won't happen if she isn't there to give the workshops!

- Martha must call all of the advertising customers for the magazine or they won't be as willing to advertise!
- Martha must teach every student or they won't want to come anymore!

Ah, vanity! As William Penn said, "To be a man's own fool is bad enough; but the vain man is everybody's." There is nothing so vain as assuming nobody can do it as well as you do!

I still struggle with delegating, but here are a few tips on how I make it work. After reading my myths and how I overcame them, please make a list of your own myths and how you will overcome them!

Delegate to Your Team

In my earlier books, I wrote every word. I sewed every stitch and put the sample in front of the artist at each step. Now, if I wrote every word we certainly wouldn't publish three to five books per year. I have artists who can draw how-to steps without having every stitch put down in front of them because they have major sewing skills in addition to art skills. I have an individual who writes much better instructions than I could ever write, and she has a staff to help her when necessary.

Ask for Help

Ask the individual if he/she is willing to do a certain task. I find I get the best results when I clearly let my team member know that I would normally do the task myself, but I have other work that is pressing. Then let them know that you think they can certainly do the job as well or better than you can.

Give Others Responsibility

There are all kinds of tasks that others can do easily as well as you: make phone calls, receive messages, prepare reports—the list goes on and on. Giving others responsibility makes them grow and makes them more valuable members of your team. Let someone screen calls and make appropriate decisions. Let them call people back after checking with you, if this is necessary.

Hire Good People

If you hire good people, you can delegate. I hire the best accounting people in my business and the best accounting firm outside my business. I need to know the big picture about our finances each month and perhaps each week. I depend on the team to make good decisions and to bring me into it when I'm needed or for necessary major changes. I always keep up with sales by the month and major financial challenges. Other than that, I just check monthly for sales, trends, and other details that interest me. I have a wonderful staff who track cost and quality at all times.

More Great Tips on Delegating

- Delegating can be started on a small scale.
- As soon as you trust certain individuals, expand the scale.
- Always ask, don't demand, that they do extra tasks.
- Brag on jobs well done. Go out of your way to compliment people.
- Keep close tabs on other people's deadline schedules. This is necessary for your peace of mind as well as for their focusing on dates when there is a lot to do.
- If help is needed, have private meetings to determine how you can help or who you need to bring in to help. I do not hesitate to get help for an individual if the deadline can't be met or if he/she has bitten off more than he/she can chew.
- Have private meetings frequently, if only for five minutes, to write down where each person is on the task that has been delegated.
- If I delegate a task to an individual, and nothing is done about it or it is simply forgotten, that is usually called

laziness or incompetence. Evaluate that person carefully. Keep an eye on him/her. Document every task that
doesn't get done and keep a dated file with the details
of incompetencies. Bring these incompetencies to the
person's attention and ask if there is any particular reason
that the jobs haven't been done. Ask if he or she needs
help.

- Brag on jobs well done. Go out of your way to compliment people. (Yes, I'm repeating this from above. I want
to make sure you understand it is more important to find
out what they are doing right and brag on them, than to
look for what they are doing wrong.)

Creating Family as Your Business Team

Enlisting Phone Help

Even if you don't run your business from your home, you
will have business calls at home. A client calling your home
office or your home and hearing, "Yeah? He isn't here now; call
back," does not enhance your image. Commission incentives
for your family team are a big motivator toward business professionalism, but praise is always best. Tell others how good
your family members are at answering the phone when your
family can overhear you.

- Explain about the projects you are working on. Get them
excited about helping you to serve your customers.
- Teach your family a pleasant business greeting to use in
answering the phone. Even the very young can be taught
the value of business manners and how vital they are to
your family and well-being. When Lilly was only five, her
mother taught her to answer the phones by saying,
"Walter's residence, Lilly speaking. May I help you?"
Callers were delighted that an obviously tiny person

would be so professional. They would giggle, give a nice compliment, and ask for Mommy or Daddy. If a message needed to be taken, Lilly would call the babysitter. Lessons learned early can become an asset to your children's futures.

- "_____ (your business name), how may I help you?"
- Teach them to take messages. Never ask someone if they mind calling back later; they mind!
- Teach them the words that convey concern to every customer: "She very much wants to speak to you about this. She will call you back as soon as possible."
- Teach them to close with, "Thank you for calling us!"

Balancing Family

As I said before, if you turn your hobby into a business, it will stop being a hobby. One of the first things to suffer will be your family. My family hasn't had as many home-cooked meals as they deserved. Joe and I have spent a lot of time apart, and I don't do lovely little dinner parties for eight anymore. I don't get to spend as much time with my eight grandchildren as I would like.

During the high school years of our youngest child, Joanna, I missed some events that she would have liked for me to have attended. I turned down many invitations to teach all over the world and to present at major shows because I didn't want to travel and leave my young family. Until Joanna was in high school, I made my family time my priority as far as my being near Huntsville. Of course, they were always my top priority after God.

Joe and I decided after Joanna entered high school that it would be all right for me to travel about two times per month. During the two weeks I was home I put all of my energy into them, especially evenings and weekends. Joanna and her dad developed a wonderful relationship during that time.

Previously, we had done so many things together that Dad wasn't too involved in her life. They became best friends during her high school years. My mother says that my traveling was the best thing that ever happened to the two of them since I tended to hover over Joanna probably too much.

Planning your family into your life takes hard work. If you only do your business when it's easy, you won't do it. Hard work for the business and hard work for the family must go hand in hand.

Plan ways to let them know they are loved and important. The easiest way is to get them excited about your new project. But, if they can't, or don't want to, find ways to keep them feeling warm and loved while you are busy.

Firing

As I approach my seventeenth year as a business owner, I am more realistic about staffing problems. In the beginning I would often keep people on who should have been fired. I just kept thinking, "I will make this team great if it kills me!" Well, I almost died! (Actually I heard that from the famous and brilliant speaker Jim Rohn, but it so aptly fit my feelings I now use it as my own! Sorry, Jim.)

If a staff can't lead or follow, they are simply roadblocks! Laziness, bad attitudes, poor salesmanship, poor quality work, working outside deadlines, and general sloppiness have no place in your business. The attitude of "getting on the employment line" is one that isn't well received in my life. Small businesses have too few employees as it is and there isn't room for any "I deserve my job" attitudes from employees. This is a difficult economy and there are many people out there who are willing to work.

Problem Solving

Dreams of being an entrepreneur are so lovely . . . simple . . . peaceful, I dreamed I would open my doors and a few people would casually come in all day long. I would sip tea with them, cut their materials, and offer suggestions. I would have time to sit and smock with some of them. Then I would hire good teachers to teach the classes.

. . . and then we opened the doors for real!

Those dreams popped the first day as business boomed! I desperately needed help to serve the customers during the busy part of the day. I quickly had to hire an assistant.

The dream was lovely; the reality was thrilling! We can learn from problems. Problems have their own rewards. When you finally find the solutions and have those solutions working, there is a secret joy and excitement.

When things go wrong, don't go with them! Your team will rush to pull harder on the oars if your hand is calmly and unflinchingly grasping the rudder. When you panic and look around in confusion, the whole boat flounders.

Problem solving, and the skill with which you go about it, makes the difference in the way your customers and your staff offer their love and loyalty. Fighting the difficult challenges offered by life each day is the perfect opportunity to build relationships. "Fight" with passion—passion to build, not to burn.

A smooth sea never made a skillful mariner.
—English proverb

Problem-Solving System

I am grateful for all my problems. After each one was overcome, I became stronger and more able to meet those that were still to come. I grew in my difficulties.
—J. C. Penney, U.S. businessman

When I approach a problem, I am most successful when I put **G**od first, become **R**esilient, take **A**ction, get **C**reative, and employ **E**nthusiasm. I suggest to you and your team to take the following steps with an attitude of GRACE:

- Pray for God's guidance.
- Strip yourself of preconceived opinions and prejudices.
- State the problem as you see it.
- Get a consensus from your team that the problem is as stated, and make adjustments as needed.
- Assemble all the facts.
- Make a list of several solutions.
- Have your team make a list of the pros and cons of each solution.
- A good problem statement often includes: (1) What do we know? (2) What don't we know? and (3) What are we looking for?

Allow the Unconscious to Solve It

You often get a better hold upon a problem by going away from it for a time and dismissing it from your mind altogether. My precious God has been the best problem solver in my life. Through prayer I get the right guidance. When I try to make decisions on my own, they tend to fall flat. I tell myself when problems occur, which is daily of course, that God is sovereign, he is in control, and he doesn't make mistakes. With those three statements, I pray about his will in fixing things. He knows what I need long before I know that I need it.

CHAPTER FIFTEEN

How to Be Passionate about Your Business When the Honeymoon Is Over

What do you do when the excitement of your business begins to fade? When your financial difficulties set in, when people are rude and unkind, when your family does not support your dream? This section will give you some thoughts to help deal with those blah days when your enthusiasm wanes and the hard times hit.

When Thomas Edison invented the lightbulb, he is said to have tried more than 2,000 experiments before he got it to work. A young reporter asked Mr. Edison how he felt—to have failed so many times! Edison said, "I never failed once. I invented the light bulb. It just happened to be a 2,000-step process."

Believe in Your Dream

Kathi Dunn loved doing art from the time she was a small girl. Art became a hobby as she ventured into and out of more "serious" career pursuits—X-ray technician, college instructor, sales, consulting, and speaking. One day, when she realized she was in a failing marriage and had to find a way to pull herself up by her bootstraps and start over, Kathi asked herself what it was that really fueled her fire. It was her art; the time had come no longer to toy with it as a hobby but to make a serious commitment to it. As a single parent in her thirties, she went back to school full-time to pursue a degree in fine art and advertising design. A month after graduating summa cum laude, she started her own business against all odds and with very little support. Today her award-winning company, Dunn + Associates, is recognized nationally as a leader in design for speakers, authors, and publishers, with clients like Anthony Robbins, Ken Blanchard, Dottie and Lilly Walters, Prentice-Hall, and Simon & Schuster. "The secret of my success is knowing without a doubt that my art is my passion. It's easy to overcome obstacles when you're absolutely driven to do what you love to do and stay committed to that path. When things get tough, I remind myself 'I am an artist who also happens to own a design firm, and who also happens to be a mother, wife, and friend.'"

Fake It Till You Make It!

So, your personal enthusiasm is gone? The 'ole spirit left you? What to do? Play a game with me. Think of something dismal . . . go ahead . . . I'll wait. Once you get that rotten, depressed thought in your mind, try singing the old Disney tune, "Zip-a-dee-doo-da! Zip-a-dee-a!" You automatically feel better! It is just amazing that when you pretend to be enthusiastic, you will be enthusiastic.

This is a very simplistic approach to NLP, neuro-linguistic programming—an interesting and excellent "new" program, which (in loose terms) simply means, "You are what you think."

Sometimes your hurt goes right into your soul. This simple system can be great even then. Sometimes it takes love.

Sometimes It Takes Love to Forgive

On Good Friday in 1986 I was at a doll show in California having the time of my life introducing all of the doll dressers to heirloom sewing, French lace, and Swiss batiste. I had just published my second book, *French Sewing by Machine*, which featured my daughter, Joanna, and my beloved sister Mary's two wonderful children, Anna and precocious little seven-year-old Al on the front cover. I got a call in the middle of the night. Al had been hit by a drunk driver.

To me, life's greatest tragedy is losing a child. Al was just like my own son or grandson. Nothing in my life had ever hurt like this did. My whole family was dying on the inside. Mary's pastor at First Methodist Church in Montgomery was at the hospital when they brought me from the airport. After I arrived, he took us into the chapel to ask God's mercy to get us through this tragic time. After some time of weeping, praying, and talking, he said, "I hope you are going to be able to forgive this man." He read Matthew 6:14–15, "For if you forgive men when they sin against you, your heavenly Father will also forgive you. But if you do not forgive men their sins, your Father will not forgive your sins." That was probably the hardest forgiving that we have ever done, but we prayed to forgive him. But, as God promises, with our forgiveness comes his mercy to heal our hearts and carry on.

I felt God was telling me to do something positive with my pain. Now I use my seminars as an opportunity to ask people to get involved in taking drunk drivers off the road in their communities. I ask them to support Mothers Against Drunk Driving, an organization that I believe has had a great impact in changing drunk driving laws in this country. I also use my business contacts to inform people about organ donation. You see, Al's family chose to donate his organs. Because of Al, eighteen people had a chance to live. That helped our pain a great deal. As difficult as it is when we are faced with horrible situations, we can find ways to turn them into the positive. All of living in GRACE is centered in this.

Through Christ, I was able to forgive the man who murdered our precious little Al. Certainly through Christ, I can forgive employees' mistakes and other deeds in my business. I think forgiveness in the business world is necessary to maintain a positive attitude. I don't want to hold any grievances in my heart against anyone.

You Get Out What You Put In

We cannot hold a torch to light another's path without brightening our own.
—Ben Sweetland

Let me tell you what my Grandmother Dicus told me (which I just bet is what your relatives tried to pound into your young mind). "You get out of life what you put in." Or, if she were really miffed with me, she'd pull out, "As ye sow, so shall ye reap!"

Zig Ziglar tells the story of a young boy who in mid-tantrum ran out of his home. At the hillside he shouted into the valley, "I hate you, I hate you, I hate you!" An echo shouted his words back at him! Frightened, he ran back and told his mother there was a mean little boy in the valley saying he hated him. His mother took him back to the hillside and told him to shout, "I love you, I love you!" Ah, it seemed a nice little boy was in the valley saying, "I love you, I love you."[10]

Even when your heart is heavy, or you are discouraged, send out the messages of enthusiasm. Soon they will echo back to you a bit stronger than what you sent out. Before long you, and those around you, will find themselves walking lighter, faster, and with passion.

Surround Yourself with Enthusiasm

Whatever you put in your mind comes out as words, thoughts, and actions. Your mind tends to absorb things from the environment around it. If you surround yourself with negative people, you will become negative. Even if your life forces you to be around people who are dismal (perhaps because of your current job), take charge of the other areas from which your mental computer is absorbing data: the music you listen to, the television you watch, the books you read, the friends you socialize with. I find my main source of comfort in hectic times to be my Bible.

Nobody ever outgrows Scripture; the book widens and deepens with our years.
—Charles H. Spurgeon (1834–1892),
English preacher and author

Create an Enthusiasm Group

Enthusiasm groups can keep you inspired and on track. Benjamin Franklin created a small group of like-minded individuals who wished to seek solutions to various issues of importance and offer possible solutions. It met once a week, posing a question or problem each time and then accepting the reports of the members the following week after their reflection and research into the problem and possible solutions.

Bring positive thinkers into your life. You might actually assign one of them to help you be more positive by reminding you when you slip into negative thoughts.

I Don't Believe in "Happy"

I have never met people more desperately unhappy than those seeking to be happy. As John Stuart Mill, the English philosopher and economist, said in 1873, "Ask yourself whether you are happy, and you cease to be so."[11] One of our pastors, Dr. Dick Thomassian, says, "Don't look for happiness, because happiness depends on happenings. Look for joy because that comes from our Lord." I love to experience the joy of knowing Christ as my personal Savior. I love the peace that comes from him alone, and I love knowing that joy is truly lasting because it is based on God's presence within me. I know that I can feel joy no matter what kind of trouble faces me. Happiness is so temporary since circumstances change sometimes by the minute in my life and that of my business.

I am not happy, I am cheerful. There's a difference. A happy woman has no cares at all. A cheerful woman has cares, but has learned how to deal with them.

—Beverly Sills (1929–),
American soprano opera star,
author of *Bubbles*

Believe in Life, Not Stress

I used to believe in stress. At one time my vision of how my life might look when I became truly successful was: me sitting in my posh office sipping a Diet Coke. My trusted employee brings the final set of proof sheets for the upcoming issue of the magazine or new book. When she arrives I languidly glance at them and nod my approval before I pick up the phone to check on other aspects of my business that my able and ample staff is attending to.

"Dorothy, honey! Wake up! It's Auntie Em."

Let me tell what my life is *really* like today. "Financial stress" takes on a whole new meaning when you start working in the millions. Deadlines haunt my dreams. I travel at least part of thirty-five weeks in any year. I need to plan new directions for the company and make sure the old plans are working. I always have jet lag, it seems. I try to do some things with my gorgeous husband, my seventy-nine-year-old mother, my grandchildren, and my children. I have Diet Cokes but no leisure anything when I am in my office.

Yes, I believed in stress!

Then, in Chicago, one of my seminar students changed my life. At lunch I sat down beside a lovely lady. As we got to know each other a little better, I found out that she was a managing physician for a practice of ninety other physicians.

"Oh my, you must have the most stressful job in Chicago!"

"I don't believe in stress."

"Uuh . . ." was my first witty reply. After picking my thoughts up off the floor, I asked, "What do you mean?"

She explained that stress is a state of maladjustment. We all choose what we do with our lives. We choose how we handle those events in our lives. It doesn't matter what business or occupation one is in, that person can be "stressed out." Recently she had taken her two children to buy shoes and she asked where her usual salesperson was. The answer was, "He had to quit. The stress was too much for him." How stressful can selling shoes be? As stressful as one wants it to be.

After that I began to simply eliminate the word *stress* from my life. I just don't believe in stress; I believe in life. I believe life is fast. I believe my Father will not send me any task that he and I together cannot handle. I just call it by another name, and it looks a great deal better than it did before.

When people say, "I don't know how you do what you do," I reply, "I have a loving God, a wonderful supportive husband, and a fabulous staff. I pray a lot. With all of that help, I don't have much trouble keeping up." I just believe that I am not stressed. It works.

OK, OK, it doesn't work all the time. When I feel really down, which isn't often, I go get some professional help from a Christian counselor. After a few hours, I am back on target again and I try to wipe negative words out of my vocabulary. But sometimes I want to scream, "I can't stand the stress any longer!" Joe allows me this privilege and I appreciate his understanding. The difference is now I don't allow those words to cross my mind often. I just think of my physician friend in Chicago who taught me this valuable lesson.

*This is true joy of life—being used for a purpose that
is recognized by yourself as a mighty one . . . instead
of being a feverish, selfish little clod of ailment and
grievances, complaining that the world will not devote
itself to making you happy.*
> —George Bernard Shaw (1856–1950),
> Anglo-Irish playwright and critic

People Skills with GRACE

When I find myself becoming a bit too smug with my success, I hear God's voice saying, "Martha, remember the entire population of the universe, with only one tiny exception, is composed of others." It is the blessing of God, the people you work with and their loyalty, and your personal likability and hard work that will make you a legendary success. You build these skills by traveling on your journey with them, striving to walk in GRACE.

God: First in all things.

*Any concern too small to be turned into a prayer is
too small to be made into a burden.*
> —Corrie ten Boom, prisoner of war in a
> Nazi concentration camp, author of
> *The Hiding Place*

Resilience: Get up when you're down. You conquer by continuing.

*In this world you will have trouble. But take heart!
I have overcome the world.*
> —John 16:33

Action: It is not enough to dream; wake up and work at it!

> *It has been said that success can come only*
> *working half days. Choose either twelve*
> *hours per day that you like.*
> —Martha Pullen

Creativity: Allow the unusual to happen. God gives creative minds for us to use.

> *Be brave enough to live life creatively. The creative is*
> *the place where no one else has ever been. You have to*
> *leave the city of your comfort and go into the*
> *wilderness of your intuition. You can't get there by bus,*
> *only by hard work and risk and by not quite knowing*
> *what you're doing. What you'll discover will be*
> *wonderful. What you'll discover will be yourself.*
> —Alan Alda, American actor

Enthusiasm: Allow the spirit of excitement to fill you and spread to your friends. It is contagious and delightfully enriching.

> *I will exalt you, my God the King;*
> *I will praise your name for ever and ever.*
> *Every day I will praise you*
> *and extol your name for ever and ever.*
> *Great is the LORD and most worthy of praise;*
> *his greatness no one can fathom.*
> —Psalm 145:1–3

CONCLUSION

Without God as the head of my life, I would not have achieved a single success that I claim today. He has opened doors that my eyes couldn't even begin to see. Asking God to guide me has been more effective for my business success than anything I could have done on my own.

I have no doubt that you have to believe in yourself and work hard to accomplish your dreams; however, I know that God has the keys to doors that I never dreamed would open. Working hand in hand with him has been the true miracle of the success of this business. All of the glory for all we have achieved goes to God and God alone.

When I find things are getting tough—and the more success-ful you are, the greater the challenges will be—I reach out for the touch of the Master's hand.

But those who hope in the LORD will renew their strength. They will soar on wings like eagles; they will run and not grow weary, they will walk and not be faint.
—Isaiah 40:31

With the touch of the Master's hand, perhaps you will turn your hobby to profit. I would love to hear from you. (Martha Pullen, *You Can Make Money from Your Hobby*; 518 Madison St., Huntsville, AL 35801.) May God bless and keep you as you begin pursuing your dreams of a hobby-based business.

ENDNOTES

1. Ralph Waldo Emerson (1803–82), U.S. essayist, poet, philosopher. The Conduct of Life, "Worship" (1870).
2. These are units within bigger agencies that support new business growth, attract new ventures to the area, and attempt to keep local employers from moving away. You will find Economic Development offices usually within the following organizations: state governments, city and county governments, major utilities who want to foster economic activity in their area of service, multi-jurisdictional co-operatives, Housing and Redevelopment Authorities (usually funded through HUD).
3. Ray Como, http://www.raycomo.com.
4. John Amatt, from an interview for the book.
5. Lilly and Dottie Walters, *Speak and Grow Rich* (New York: Prentice-Hall, 1998, Simon & Schuster, 1998). Reprinted with permission.
6. Ann Ball, from an interview for the book.
7. *Sky*, Delta Airline in-flight magazine, October 1995.
8. Lilly Walters, *Secrets of Successful Speakers—How You Can Motivate, Captivate, and Persuade* (New York: McGraw Hill, 1993).
9. John Morreall, "Humor," *International Journal of Humor Research* (Walter De Gruyter, 1991), 364.
10. Zig Ziglar, *See You at the Top* (New York: Pelican, 1978), 103.
11. John Stuart Mill (1806–73), autobiography (1873).